ROMARE BEARDEN

celebrating the victory

ROMARE BEARDEN

celebrating the victory

by Myron Schwartzman

Franklin Watts
A Division of Grolier Publishing
New York London Hong Kong Sydney
Danbury, Connecticut

For Judith and Max, my loyal and supportive family,
and for Andrew Lavender, my mentor
—M. S.

All art by Romare Bearden is © Romare Bearden Foundation/Licensed by VAGA, New York, NY.

Photographs ©: Barnett-Aden Collection of African-American Art, Florida Endowment for Higher Education: 72 bottom; Bridgeman Art Library International Ltd., London/New York: 71 bottom (CH99185 Violin, Bottle and Glass, 1913, oil, collage and charcoal on canvas by Pablo Picasso/Christie's Images/Private Collection); Corbis-Bettmann: 32, 35; Cordier & Ekstrom Gallery, New York: 111 top (Courtesy of Maya Angelou), 66 bottom, 108 bottom, 109 bottom, 111 bottom (Private Collection), 110 bottom (Private Collection, Scarsdale, NY/Photo by Geoffrey Clements), 65 top, 66 top, 67, 70 top; Francis Lee: 57; Mint Museum of Art: 86 (Collection of Wadsworth Atheneum Hartford, Connecticut/Geoffrey Clements Photography), 108 top (Museum purchase: National Endowment for the Arts Matching Fund and the Charlotte Debutante Club Fund), cover center; Museum of Modern Art, New York: 71 top; New York Public Library Picture Collection: 59 (Art Digest 21/Dec 1 1946); New York University Archives: 45; Private Collection: cover top, 65 bottom, 69; Romare Bearden Foundation.: 68 bottom, 70 bottom, 105 top, 106, 107, 112; Rousmanière Alston and Aida Winters: 17, 22, 23, 26, 50; Sam Shaw: 9; Sheldon Ross Gallery, Birmingham, MI.: cover bottom, 110 top (Private Collection, Southfield, MI.), 68 top, 105 bottom; The Cleveland Museum of Art: 109 top (Mr. and Mrs. William H. Fund, 85.41); Whitney Museum of American Art/©Estate of Stuart Davis, Licensed by VAGA, New York, NY.: 72 top (Photo by Geoffrey Clements).

Library of Congress Cataloging-in-Publication Data
Schwartzman, Myron.
    Romare Bearden : celebrating the victory / by Myron Schwartzman.
    p. cm.
    Includes bibliographical references and index.
    Summary: Recounts the life of the twentieth-century African-American collage artist who used his southern childhood, New York City, jazz, and Paris to influence his bold and meaningful art.
    ISBN 0-531-11387-6
    1. Bearden, Romare, 1911–1988—Juvenile literature. 2. Afro-American artists—Biography—Juvenile literature. [1. Bearden, Romare, 1911–1988. 2. Artists. 3. Afro-Americans—Biography.] I. Title.
N6537.B4S38 1999
709'.2—dc21
[B]
                            98-45806

CIP
AC

© 1999 by Myron Schwartzman
Printed in the United States of America.
1 2 3 4 5 6 7 8 9 10 R 08 07 06 05 04 03 02 01 00 99

Acknowledgments

I am most grateful to Edythea Ginis Selman, an extraordinarily bright, gifted, and tenacious woman who is not only a terrific agent but also a real friend.

At Franklin Watts, it has been my good fortune to work with Dana M. Rau, the kind and wonderful editor every writer wishes for.

Contents

Meeting Romare

Bearden in front of New York's
Apollo Theater in 1952

November 1978. Romare Bearden, often called the Dean of
African-American artists, was at the height of his career and
enjoying every moment of it. I walked through an exhibition
of twenty-eight of his collages installed at the Cordier and
Ekstrom Gallery in New York City. The collages were paintings that combined cut and pasted paper, bits of photographs, pieces of burlap, wallpaper, and paint, placed one
on top of the other to make something new, something different from just the sum of their parts. With brilliant colors
in surprising combinations that seemed to break many of
the rules of painting, they glowed like suns.

A year earlier, *The New Yorker* magazine had published a
profile of Bearden, tracing his long struggle from his birthplace in Charlotte, North Carolina, to Harlem, Pittsburgh,

Paris, and back to New York in the process of perfecting his art. The idea of a profile, or biography of a life in art, gave rise to Bearden's idea of a series on that theme. It was entitled *Profile/Part I: The Twenties*. Bearden and his friend Albert Murray, a novelist and formidable writer on jazz, had collaborated on a series of short narratives, which Bearden had written on the gallery walls below the collages. What the collages accomplished visually, the words replayed in the imagination.

Beneath the first collage, entitled *School Bell Time*, was the memory: "Once it was mid-September again, it was back to Miss Pinkney and books, blackboards, rulers and fingernail inspection." In the collage, a teacher is ringing a bell which, on closer inspection, turns out to be the reverse image of a huge school bell on top of a barnlike school building.

Next to that large collage was a small gem called *Miss Bertha and Mr. Seth*. Miss Bertha stands with her huge left hand holding a cane, and Mr. Seth, straw hat protecting him from the Carolina sun, holds an infant that could only have been a grandchild. Miss Bertha is smiling and Mr. Seth looks solemn and proud, as if they were posing for a photographer. The narrative read: "They rented a house from my grandfather."

Farther along the gallery wall were two collages devoted to Bearden's recollection of Maudell Sleet, a woman he knew as a little boy growing up in Mecklenburg County. In a small collage bursting with the rich color of flowers, an African-American woman with a blue dress and yellow sun hat sits on the earth in front of her cabin. The memory was: "I can still smell the flowers she used to give us and still taste the blackberries." The title was *Maudell Sleet's Magic Garden*. Next to that was *Sunset and Moonrise with Maudell Sleet*, a huge collage. Standing between a white full moon rising and a burnt-orange sun setting, a woman with gigantic, outsized hands looks directly at the viewer.

Beneath the collage was the memory: "When her husband died she worked the farm, most of the time by herself."

The two *Maudell Sleets* look unlike each other, photographically speaking, but they were faithful to Bearden's memory. As he told me later: "Since it was a profile, I was talking about remembrances, and actual people—actual people but not photographs of them. You know, like Maudell Sleets. I've done her about two or three times; and each time the facial characteristics are different: I wouldn't recognize her as the same woman one for the other, but it's all right for my *memory . . .*"

Trains were also a subject that steamed through these collages like reminders of time and place. *Daybreak Express,* for instance, depicts a nude stretched out on a bed, still sleeping while outside the open window of her cabin, like a landscape all by itself, a locomotive pulls a steaming express along an open field. The narrative read: "You could tell not only what train it was but also who the engineer was by the sound of the whistle."

Next to that on the gallery wall was *The Afternoon Northbound,* in which a long train wends its way under an open sky set off by a spread-winged hawk in flight. The narrative read: "There were no bad trains, but everybody used to think of the passenger expresses as good trains."

Next to that was *Sunset Limited.* In it, a woman holds a baby, a horse and chickens feed lazily in the foreground, and a train moves across a field beneath a spectacular, red-orange ball of sun. The memory was: "The last time I saw Liza was down at the station when I left for Pittsburgh on the 5:13."

Finally I came upon *Moonlight Express.* A nude sits on a cloth next to a bucket she will bathe in, attended by a grandmotherly woman. Behind them, a train steams under a full moon. This narrative read: "Sometimes at night I used to dream of being the one who was running the train." By daybreak, afternoon, sunset, and moonlight, Bearden was recalling the trains that filled his world, whether he was still asleep in the morning or dreaming at night.

Among these Mecklenburg, North Carolina, themes important to the profile was music, both secular and sacred. My eye was captured by a small work called *Country Band*, in which a group of men in dungarees and straw hats play bass drum, guitar, and trombone, with a little boy watching. The memory: "You could see them every Saturday afternoon on the street corner, and sometimes they still played at picnics and baseball games." No less a part of the countryside, the counterpart to this folk jazz was the church. *Dinner before Revival Meeting* depicts a group seated around a picnic table with the revival tent in the background, and it carried a memory about food: "I remember the food—most of all, though, I remember the dasher-turned ice cream." Next to it, in *Holiness Church Revival*, a country preacher holds a woman in religious transport, but this memory was all about music: "You could hear the tambourines from Holiness Church as far away as you could hear the dance bands."

Next to these, the small, delightful *Spring Revival Baptism* shows a group immersing converts in a stream ("With the Baptist converts, they had to go under water"). A gigantic hand is about to pour baptismal water from the stream over a child with upraised arms. That hand, and each of the other figures in the collage, is larger than the locomotive train pulling into a station in the foreground. Clearly, the parts of a Bearden collage were sized according to their importance.

Two more biblical collages in this group, *Expulsion from Paradise* and *Joshua at Jericho,* showed the subjects of some popular sermons. As might be expected from a long artistic tradition of the subject, in *Paradise,* Adam and Eve stand on either side of an apple tree around which a snake is coiled. Then they are shown being expelled from the garden by an angel holding an upraised sword. What upset one's preconception was that all the figures were black (as was entirely natural in the imagination of a black congregation hearing a sermon). The narrative was continuous: "The church was always filled when people knew Reverend Russell was going to preach about Adam and Eve and the apple." Beneath *Joshua*: ". . . and the same was true when the subject was Joshua and the Battle at Jericho."

After the Mecklenburg County collages came a section called *Pittsburgh Memories*. While Bearden's North Carolina skies had glowed with orange-red suns and large white moons, his Pittsburgh skies were fiery red from the steel mills. In *Mill Hand's Lunch Bucket*, for instance, a family group sits around a breakfast table, while a young mill hand descends the stairs to go to work. His huge hand reaches for the lunch bucket, waiting for him on top of a table. But it's the fire-red cap of the mother, who stands serving breakfast, that catches the eye. Her cap leads one's eye to the window—a steel-mill landscape all by itself. Railroad tracks, chimneys, and clouds of smoke emerging from a gigantic furnace fill the scene. The narrative reads: "The mills went 24 hours a day with three 8-hour shifts."

Next came *Allegheny Morning Sky*, which also depicts a woman preparing to serve breakfast. No one is sitting at the table yet, though a figure is seen in the bedroom at the center back. The eye is drawn to the rectangular landscape in the window at the left. Again, it is a scene of steel mills and chimneys. The sky is fire—orange-white cloud fire set off against a deeper fire. The narrative came from a youngster's imagination: "I used to look at the sky and think of story-book dragons."

The profile exhibition was dazzling, and I returned several times. The last time was on the closing day of the exhibition, when the collages were to come down. I had arranged to meet Albert Murray at the gallery that day, and he said he'd introduce me to Romare Bearden. I was scared. Why I was scared is a mystery to me, even today, although I resolved to go through with the introduction.

Much later, I found that I was not unique. The playwright August Wilson, who found his artistic mentor in Bearden, once stood in front of Bearden's walk-up at 357 Canal Street trying to summon the courage to knock. In the end, he didn't. In every other way, however, Wilson knocked at the door, and Bearden opened it. He unlocked many artistic secrets, showing Wilson a sure road and charting a path with clear signposts and directions. Wilson wrote, for instance, that Seth and Bertha, two characters in his play *Joe Turner's Come and Gone* had come from *Miss Bertha and Mr. Seth*. The play itself had been inspired by *Mill Hand's Lunch Bucket*.

As I look back on our first meeting, it seems entirely natural that my primary desire was to become invisible, to hide behind Albert Murray, or to walk out the gallery doors and just keep walking. Bearden was busy writing the titles of the collages on their masonite backings. Bearden and his friend Murray greeted each other and began talking; I was becoming a bit less terrified. Bearden was a heavyset, 210-pound (95-kg), light-skinned African-American man with the look of a Russian truck driver and the voice of a hip, Southern jazz musician. It turned out that as rooted, steady, and giantlike as he was, Bearden was light and quick, both physically and intellectually.

Then I was introduced. "Yeah, how are you?" Bearden said to me, in a formal yet not unfriendly way. "I've read some of your work." I wanted to die on the spot from embarrassment, but at least that was all Bearden said.

Bearden went back to work and Albert Murray gave me his own special tour of the collages remaining on the gallery walls.

He also showed me the catalogs of Bearden's prior shows, "The Odysseus Collages" (1977), "Of the Blues" (1975), and "Of the Blues: Second Chorus" (1976)—and Murray's introductory essay to "Of the Blues" in an open catalog in the display case! In the street, as Murray and I parted, I sailed off on a cloud.

2

Mecklenburg Morning

Romare Bearden made his art sing on canvas. He created the visual definition of jazz, as if he played the red-hot brassy ragtime figures of a great trumpet player, or the oh-so-cool blue, elegantly composed chords of a piano legend. Just as the great blues-band sections call and answer each other, trading "riffs" or musical phrases with each new line of blues, so Bearden called and recalled his life experiences in his art.

Bearden spent his earliest years in Charlotte, North Carolina, hearing locomotives steam past his great-grandparents' home, their lonely whistles piercing the air night and day. As a little boy walking among cotton fields and visiting Cherokee Indian lands, Romare formed lasting impressions of Southern black life. Ultimately, he painted his own story—that of all people—with such genius that it became a celebration of the human condition.

In this family photograph from 1912, young Romare sits in the arms of his great-grandfather, Henry B. Kennedy, who stands beside his wife Rosa and daughter Rosa Catherine (Cattie).

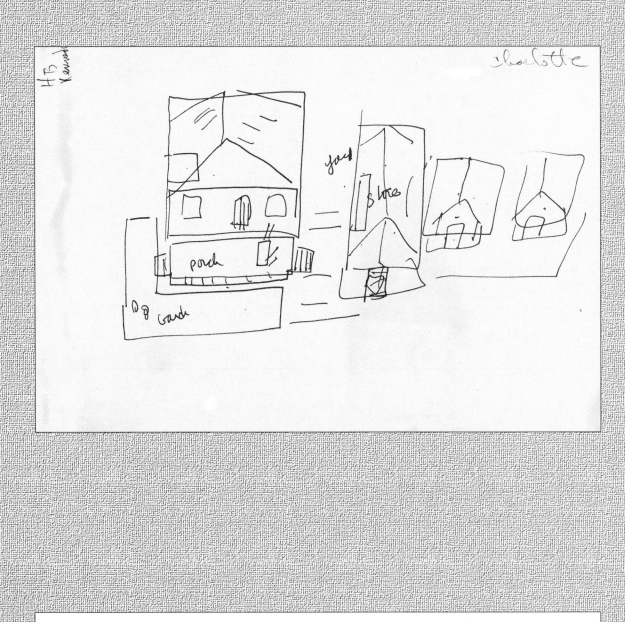

Bearden's sketch of his birthplace, the home of his great-grandparents in Charlotte, North Carolina. A yard separates the corner house from his great-grandfather's grocery store and rental houses.

Romare was born on the morning of September 2, 1911, the only child of Bessye and Howard Bearden, in the home of Howard's grandparents—Henry B. and Rosa Kennedy. They owned a beautiful corner house and grocery store in Charlotte, the seat of Mecklenburg County.

The baby was named Fred Romare Howard Bearden. These names show the respect Romare's father Howard felt for his grandfather, H. B. Kennedy. Fred Romare (ROM-ree), a friend of H. B. Kennedy's, was a harness maker in Joplin, Missouri, who had no children. Thus, Romare was a last name used as a first name for Bearden. He was baptized at the Episcopal Church of St. Michael and All Angels. In later life, Romare dropped the name Fred but kept his father's name Howard as his middle name.

Like other black people who put down roots in Charlotte after the Civil War, Romare's great-grandparents enjoyed relative freedom of opportunity. Born into slavery, they accomplished much since the Emancipation Proclamation of 1863. When Henry and Rosa married in 1863, he was eighteen and she was sixteen. Their only child, Rosa Catherine (Cattie) Kennedy was born two years later.

Henry and Rosa worked for the family of Dr. Joseph Wilson, a Presbyterian minister in Columbia, South Carolina. Dr. Wilson's son Woodrow became the twenty-eighth president of the United States in 1913, two years after Romare's birth. Woodrow Wilson was twelve or thirteen years old when Henry and Rosa worked for the Wilsons.

When Romare learned to read, his great-grandfather sat him in a special chair and showed him a booklet published in Charlotte celebrating fifty years of emancipation. The booklet described his great-grandfather as one of Charlotte's prominent citizens of color, along with bishops, doctors, lawyers, and a former U.S. consul to Sierra Leone in West Africa. "Mr.

Kennedy is now using the chair that was formerly used by Dr. Wilson before President Wilson was born," the booklet said.

Henry got a job as a mail agent for the Charlotte, Columbia and Augusta Railroad, an important intercity system based in Charlotte. In the late 1870s, Rosa and their daughter Cattie joined him in Charlotte. Henry made a down payment of 100 dollars on a piece of land and several houses. He must have saved every penny, because it was an enormous sum at the time.

Henry prospered in Charlotte. In ten years, he went from being a homeowner and mail agent for the railroad to being a landowner, landlord, wood dealer, and grocer, with a store next to his corner home and several rental homes. Cattie married Richard P. Bearden, a grocer and harness maker in Charlotte, and they had three children—Anna, Harry, and Howard. Richard Bearden died in 1891, twenty years before Romare's birth. And because Romare never knew his grandfather, his great-grandfather became a grandfather to him.

Howard met Bessye Johnson Banks in Atlantic City when he went North to find work. Bessye was born in Goldsboro, North Carolina, and she grew up in Atlantic City, where she lived with her mother, Carrie, and her stepfather, George T. Banks. Bessye attended Hartshorn Memorial College in Richmond, Virginia, and graduated from Virginia Normal and Industrial Institute in Petersburg. When Howard and Bessye married, he brought his new bride home to Charlotte to live with the Kennedys. Romare was born that year.

The Kennedy home was a two-story, four-room wood-frame house with a flower garden in front and a chicken coop in the back. A photograph taken about the turn of the century shows Henry and Rosa sitting on the main porch facing Graham . Street. This wide, raised porch, typical of Southern homes of the period, had a stairway at each end, a wind harp, and a swing.

A smaller porch wrapped around the other side of the house.

Diagonally opposite the Kennedy house was the home of Reverend Primus P. Alston, rector of the church where Romare was baptized. Reverend Alston established a school there called St. Michael's Training and Industrial School. Classes included home economics, cooking, and sewing for the girls, and carpentry for the boys. But it was actually an elementary school for most of the black children in that section of Charlotte. They learned reading, writing, and arithmetic as well as religion.

Southern Negro schools at that time had to emphasize industrial training to get financial help from their sponsors in the North. In 1881, Booker T. Washington was asked to run the Normal School for Negroes to be opened in Tuskegee, Alabama. He founded Tuskegee Institute, and spent his life as an educator stressing the value of industrial education for the Negro. Booker T. Washington was at the height of his influence, but to get money for a Negro school in the 1890s, you had to call it an "industrial school." Until 1907, the only public school for black children in Charlotte was the Myers School, known also as the "Jacob's Ladder School." It was so named because of the two wooden fire escapes that formed a double ramp or "ladder" on one side of the building. (Biblically, "Jacob's Ladder" refers to the ramp Jacob sees reaching up into the heavens in Genesis 28.) "Jacob's Ladder" became the title of a spiritual familiar to both black and white churchgoers in Charlotte.

Reverend Alston married a young graduate of St. Michael's School, a beautiful girl named Anna. They had three children—Wendell, Rousmanière, and Charles. In naming his second child, Reverend Alston honored his friend Edmund S. Rousmanière, dean of St. Paul's Cathedral in Boston. Her name shows the connection between the fledgling black Episcopal Church in the South and its sponsors in the North.

Howard Bearden, Romare's father

Bessye Bearden, Romare's mother

A Family Love of Art and Music

Alston's youngest child, Charles, was nicknamed "Spinky." Born in 1907, Spinky was a good friend to Romare when they lived in Charlotte, and later when they both became artists in New York City.

Several years after Reverend Alston died in 1910, the Beardens and Alstons became relatives. Romare's uncle, Harry Bearden, married Alston's widow, Anna. They had a child in 1917. Harry, an opera enthusiast, named her Aida.

The two families shared a love for music and art. Romare's Aunt Anna married a surgeon, Dr. Bullock, and settled in Greensboro, North Carolina, where she was a church organist and taught piano. Their daughter Mabel had a beautiful soprano voice and got her degree in music at Howard University. In the grocery store, next to Great-Grandfather Kennedy's home, hung his painting of *Custer's Last Stand*. Cattie's drawings included a portrait of Abraham Lincoln. Spinky was making sculptures out of Charlotte's red clay before he left for school in New York. And as for Romare, he was storing up the visual impressions that he would later transform into hundreds of Mecklenburg County collages.

Romare's earliest years were spent around his Great-Grandfather H. B. Kennedy's house. Half a block away, a train trestle and railroad bridge led to the main station. On the other side of the bridge, the Magnolia Mill processed cotton. When the machines started up in the early morning, you could hear their hum throughout the neighborhood.

Cotton was king. Almost every available acre of land was planted with cotton. Although Charlotte was not a large cotton-growing area, cotton from all over was transported there by train and by wagon. There it was weighed, put in bales, and shipped to mills where it was processed into cloth. Mills were built up and down the train line, sometimes right near the tracks.

Watching the Good Trains Go By

Romare loved to watch the trains go by the trestle not far from his window. His favorite train was the New York and Atlanta Special, which steamed southbound from Charlotte station every morning at 10 o'clock. It came back every evening at 7:30 headed for Washington, New York, and points north. That endless train, with its huge steam engine and coal car, and its Pullman drawing room sleeping cars, dining car, and parlor observation car, was a magical sight for Romare and his cousins.

They loved to hear the conductor shout out the names of the cities: "New York and Atlanta Special, boarding for Asheville, Atlanta, and Macon. Haawl . . . haboouaart!"

Many years later, it was just such trains, carrying people to special, mysterious places that Romare remembered in collage after collage. They had titles like *Watching the Good Trains Go By* (1964), *Sunset Limited* (1976), *Evening Train to Memphis* (1976), *Daybreak Express* (1978), and *The Afternoon Northbound* (1978).

Romare's early impressions were primarily visual. When he was about three years old, his great-grandfather took him to the train station. The funeral train for Mrs. Stonewall Jackson, widow of the great Confederate general, was carrying her body for burial beside her husband in Virginia. "I remember my great-grandfather carrying me and holding me up to see the railroad car with the coffin and the flowers and the soldiers."

Later, when Romare was nine or ten, he spent the summer with his great-grandparents. One of his early memories was the beauty of an orange and brown tiger lily in his great-grandfather's garden. Romare remembered going back to look at the flower every day. "But one Sunday I found it gone, and only a green stem trembling in the air like a small garter snake." Seeing his concern, Romare's great-grandfather told him that his great-grandmother had worn the flower to church. Then he

Flanked by his great-grandparents, Romare stands in front of (from left to right) his aunt Anna, his mother and father, and his grandmother Cattie in this 1917 photograph.

told Romare, "Don't worry, this is good soil and next year your tiger lily will be back once again."

This memory is a window into the impressions that had the greatest impact on Romare throughout his life. He was entranced by the beauty of flowers, gardens, and the rituals of daily life. When he felt they were in danger of being destroyed, he re-created them in his art.

When Bearden reached his peak as a master of collage, he kept returning to his childhood memories of Mecklenburg County. Although he developed his own technique and style, Bearden continued two traditions established by the artists Pablo Picasso and Georges Braque. The first was experimentation in collage—cutting and gluing painted papers, fabrics, pieces of African masks, wallpaper, and other materials one on top of the other to fuse them into new combinations. The second was cubism, a discipline Bearden used to eliminate the illusion of three-dimensional space in his collages.

Early Carolina Morning shows a seated black mother with her child standing next to her. A cat in the foreground seems to be looking straight at us, while the hot orange Carolina sun shows through a window, and the blue morning lights the squares of floorboard in a diagonal pathway through an open door. If you look closely, you can see the strong gridlike effect of rectangles moving vertically and horizontally everywhere on the flat surface. Living things, however, such as the mother, child, cat, and the rising sun are rounded, softening the geometric severity. Human beings, with their rituals and daily ceremonies, are the essence of Bearden's vision of the world. Of all the cubists, Bearden was probably the most humanistic.

3

E. C. Johnson's Blues and Eugene's Drawing Lessons

One "old old July" in the 1920s, when Romare was about ten years old, he spent the summer with his grandmother Cattie in Lutherville, Maryland, a countryside town near Baltimore. There, Romare met Mrs. Johnson. Her grandmother had been born into slavery and her baking tins had been made by a slave blacksmith. Her specialty was a watermelon cake fashioned with such expertise that you couldn't tell it from the real fruit. Mrs. Johnson hardened "seeds" of chocolate in an icy stream, placed them in a red batter, painted the top with melon stripes, and added a transparent sugar icing as a final touch. The rich white folks in Lutherville's fine old houses loved these cakes, and Romare's job was to deliver them every Saturday morning in a little wagon.

Mrs. Johnson's husband, "E. C.," was a blind musician, famous around the countryside for his guitar-playing. One Saturday, E. C. went with Romare on his delivery route. As always, he had his guitar. When they set out, Mrs. Johnson gave Romare a pail, and promised to bake him a pie if he picked some blackberries on the way home. Along the way, E. C. held Romare's free hand, and strummed on the guitar with his right hand. After delivering the last cake and starting back, Romare noticed a good clump of blackberries off the road.

"I went with my pail to pick the berries and Mr. Johnson sat on an old tree stump and began to play his guitar. The music was strange to me and not like the church hymns or the blues, or any of the popular songs that I knew. Finally, I asked Mr. Johnson what was the music he was playing. He said 'Oh, I don't know; I'm just wandering over the chords, just as if the wind was moving my fingers.' It was fine listening to Mr. Johnson's music and picking the full ripe berries. I felt very good and I picked a beautiful rose I saw growing that I thought would please my grandmother."

E. C.'s music may have been awesome, but nobody stayed around long enough to get into conversation with him. He knew everybody's business, and inevitably had a dream about anyone he could get Romare to corral. Unfortunately, his dreams were consistently calamitous: "Oh, Mrs. Jones, I dreamt last night I saw you in that coffin just as plain," he would say. "The casket was just so nice." And finally E. C. would terrify the woman: "How are you feeling, sister? I mean, you better take care of yourself, because I dreamt about you last night."

As Bearden told the story (and he loved to tell it), when people saw E. C. coming, they scattered. "So there he was and he'd be strumming on his guitar. It was kind of out of a Greek play— leading the blind soothsayer. The little boy leads him in and he makes a dire prediction for the city."

Guitar players sound their folk blues in dozens of Bearden's collages. *Guitar Executive* is the title of two very different collages

(1967; 1979) showing guitarists Bearden associated with E. C. Johnson. He cared far more about making these images true to the way they felt to him than in capturing a photographic likeness. If they were true to feeling, they would be true as art. Many years later, Romare remembered the feeling in this poem:

What is it?
I'm trying really to remember
The clock has stopped
Now I can never know
Where the edge of my world can be
If I could only enter that old calendar
That opens to an old, old July
And learn what unknowing things know . . .

School Days in Harlem

By the time Romare was ready to start school, his parents had found an apartment on West 140th Street and Lenox Avenue in New York City. Why did they move to New York? First, Charlotte now felt far less racially welcome than it once had to Bessye and Howard. Reconstruction, the half-century era from the end of the American Civil War to Romare's birth, had been relatively good to people of color. Once, though, in the days when "Jim Crow" laws began to create separate drinking fountains, "colored only" movie theater entrances, and all the rest of the landscape of segregation, the Beardens went shopping. In the bustling center of Charlotte, a small, terrifying incident took place. Bessye, who was much lighter-skinned than Howard, left Romare in Howard's care while she stepped into a store. Howard moved a few feet away from the carriage to look into a shop window. Bessye saw the carriage unattended from inside the shop and rushed out, while at the same time Howard moved quickly toward Romare. The sight of a dark-skinned man approaching a carriage holding a very light-skinned, blond, blue-eyed child while the mother ran toward the carriage from the shop was enough. It had the momentary look to others of a kidnapping!

Another time, on a visit, Howard was stopped late at night by a white detective close to home. The detective asked Howard where he was from. "Up North," Howard said. It was the wrong choice of words. After a night spent in jail, Howard came home at dawn, told the family to dress and pack, and they left—for good.

The apartment in New York was a block away from P.S. 5, where Romare began attending school in 1917. It also overlooked a large lot extending all the way from Lenox to Seventh Avenue and from 139th Street to 140th Street. The lot was a kind of improvised park—a natural playground with trees, winding trails, small ponds, and even a cricket field where immigrants from the West Indies played on Sunday afternoons. During the late summer months in the mid-1920s, a wooden floor was laid on the flat top section of a hill made of old glacial rock that overlooked Seventh Avenue. From under a large tent called "The Garden of Joy," jazz floated on the evening air.

Romare went to elementary school and the first two years of high school in New York, except for his third- and fourth-grade years. Romare spent one year with his family in Moose Jaw, Saskatchewan, in Canada. His father, having traveled hundreds of miles to find work, got a job as a steward for the Canadian railroads. He worked on a special train that ran between Edmonton, Alberta, and Moose Jaw. Romare spent his fourth-grade year with his Grandmother Carrie in Pittsburgh.

Like Harlem itself, P.S. 5 was multiethnic. Most of the pupils were Irish, Jewish, and Italian, and a few were black. A number of students, known as "The Home Boys," wore similar uni-

Harlem, New York, in the 1920s

forms—blue pants and blue shirts. They were from the Hebrew Orphan House, then situated a bit west of Lewisohn Stadium. At the stadium, teams from City College played football, baseball, and lacrosse. On summer evenings, one could hear wonderful symphonic music, often free.

Harlem was changing year by year as its population of black people from the South swelled. The hill fronting Seventh Avenue with its playlot was dynamited and leveled so that stores, apartment houses, and P.S. 139 could be built there. Later, Romare was transferred to the new P.S. 139, along with his longtime friend Norman Lewis, who also became a painter. Romare spent the last half of the eighth grade there. At the age of twelve, he was in the first graduating class. Romare spent ninth and tenth grades at De Witt Clinton High School's annexes.

By now, Romare was thoroughly accustomed to New York City life. Still, he liked to remember "old Julys" in the South, when the blind guitar player E. C. Johnson sat the young Romare down on a tree stump in Lutherville to explain how his sound came from the wind moving his fingers over the guitar strings.

Pittsburgh Memories

A large 1984 collage by Bearden shows a brick Pittsburgh apartment house typical of the 1920s steel-mill neighborhood around it. Smokestacks belching flame rise behind its roof. On the left is the apparatus of steel production—pulleys, guy-wires and huge steel ball, a girder platform, and a locomotive pulling into the steelyard near a shanty. What is truly surprising, however, is the way Bearden has cut away the entire lower half of the brick facade to reveal an interior that could have been transported whole from a Southern parlor like that of his father's

grandparents, Henry and Rosa Kennedy, in Charlotte. A grandmother figure, her face an African mask, is seated at the right
beneath a china lamp; two women sit at a dining table; and
there's a picture on the wall, a victrola, and a straw broom lying
across a rug. A window opens onto a steel-mill landscape. Just
outside the apartment, a mill hand holding his lunch bucket is
coming down the steps. The collage, called *Pittsburgh Memories*,
is a window on a crucial part of Romare's youth, and typifies the
way his childhood impressions influenced his art.

In the early 1920s, Romare spent the summers with his
Bessye's mother Carrie and her husband, George Banks, in
Lawrenceville, Pittsburgh, near the steel mills. Carrie ran a
boardinghouse just across the road from a large steel mill.

The 1920s saw a great migration of Southern black workers
to industrial cities of the North, along with waves of immigrants from Europe. Areas such as Lawrenceville were magnets
for those seeking work. There was so much work in the mills
that laborers were trucked north from Georgia or Mississippi
and put to work immediately on gigantic blast furnaces and
assembly lines. In Pittsburgh, newly arrived Hungarian and
Czech immigrants worked side by side with black workers just
up from the South, making Pittsburgh an interesting, diverse
mix of cultures. Between 1920 and 1930, the black population of Allegheny County grew by 30,000, a 56 percent
increase.

Romare often saw trucks bringing twenty or twenty-five
men up from the South. The men needed lodgings, and
Carrie's boardinghouse was the most popular, because it was
so close to the Crucible steel mill, and also because "Miss
Carrie" was such a good cook and nurse.

From his grandmother's window, Romare could see the flames
and smoke and hear the constant bass roar of the furnaces and
the screaming factory whistles signaling shift's end. It was unbear-

The Pittsburgh steel mills, with their great columns of smoke and loud roar, made a lasting impression on Romare and greatly influenced his art.

ably hot work and the men often shed their asbestos clothing and stripped to the waist. "When the furnace doors opened," Romare said, "that flame would lick out like a burning snake's tongue and hit 'em. They were always getting scorched." Romare's grandmother rubbed the men down with lard or cocoa butter.

On the ground floor, the Banks's boardinghouse had a kitchen with several stoves and a large dining room. Single rooms for several men were on the first and second floors as well as two large dormitory rooms on the third floor, where up to twenty men slept on cots. Each floor had a single bath that ran continuously on Saturdays. During the week, there was no time for anything but work and sleep.

The men worked eight- to twelve-hour shifts five days a week and a half day on Saturday for what was then the enormous wage of about forty dollars a week. The mills never shut down, and shifts worked through the night. The factory-owners' greatest fear was a strike, because if the furnaces were shut down, they cracked and had to be rebricked.

Eugene

For Romare, this was the "time of Eugene." Eugene was a disabled boy who came to the boardinghouse one day in the summer of 1926. Romare, his cousin Spinky, and his friend Dennis were shooting marbles. Eugene just stood there silently, braces on both legs, staring at the three boys. With the sometime cruelty of young fellows, Dennis hit him. Then Romare and Spinky joined in. Romare's grandmother saw what was happening and came out with her broom to break it up. She carried Eugene into the house, and he became their friend.

Eugene took to hanging around Carrie's house, and spent a lot of time making erotic drawings on sheets of brown paper. They fascinated Romare, who had never seen anything like that before. One was a drawing of a nearby bordello, run by a woman named Sadie. Romare knew it because it was part of his newspaper route. He and his friends liked to go into Sadie's parlor because the scene was so interesting, especially the piano player off in a side room—a cigarette dangling from his mouth as his fingers stroked the keyboard in barrelhouse rags and blues.

Eugene had drawn Sadie's house with the facade cut away. Somebody had fired a pistol, and the bullet was shown going all through the house. The bullet passed by women on top of men, and women dressed only in high-gartered stockings dancing with men, and down through the ceiling into the front parlor. There stood Sadie with her purse open, and the bullet had turned into coins that were dropping into her purse.

Romare's grandmother had set up a drawing table in Romare's room, where he took daily drawing lessons from Eugene. She soon asked to see how the boys were coming along. A religious woman, she took one look, grabbed all the drawings, and threw them into the furnace. Where, she asked, had Eugene ever seen anything like this? He told her that he lived at Sadie's, where his mother worked. That night, Carrie told Sadie she was taking Eugene home to live with her and sent the boys up to Eugene's room on the top floor to get his belongings. There, Eugene showed Romare how you could see through the cracks in the floor to the rooms below.

Eugene moved into the boardinghouse, along with his pet pigeons and doves. For the next year, his mother visited him there every Sunday. They sat in the front parlor, near an old German clock with the inscription: "Every Hour Wounds. The Last One Kills." Eugene stopped drawing when he left Sadie's and died about a year later. During his short life, he had inspired Romare to learn to draw, and his influence was deep and lasting. "Lautrec would have loved him," Bearden said, "because he had that kind of an eye." He was referring to the

French artist Henri de Toulouse-Lautrec and his keen eye for Parisian nightlife and the cabaret dancers who danced the cancan.

In 1947, inspired by the *Journal of Eugène Delacroix,* written by the great nineteenth-century French master known for his use of vivid color, Bearden made a striking entry in the journal he had recently begun. He likened the artist's creative struggle to a worker's capacity to endure intense pain: "Imagine a factory whistle blowing through your spine, and consider how long you could stand this shrill discordance," he wrote. "The greater artists have been able to stand this whistle and steam blowing their insides apart a little while longer than the others. A mechanic can step up the revolutions of a motor and listen for the engine defects with his head almost in the bearings. Likewise the great artist can destroy form after form, constantly seeking the unique twist that will appear in the end as if he *owned* the entire array of shapes and colors."

The image Bearden chose to convey the intensity of the artist's struggle was, like his art, drawn directly from his own experience and then transformed. In this case, it was Bearden's early Pittsburgh memories.

4

School Days—
No Golden Rule Days

Returning to Pittsburgh in 1927 for his last two years of high school, Romare again lived with his grandmother and her husband George Banks, who had since moved to East Liberty, a neighborhood some distance from the steel mills. Romare walked to Peabody High School from his grandparents' house.

At Peabody High, he liked chemistry best and English least. "Month after month, this modifies this, that modifies that; we learned everything that would inhibit a person who actually wanted to *write* something. And double negatives! And split infinitives! But anyway it was good . . . very thorough."

Romare really liked sports, especially baseball, better than academic subjects. He tried out for the football team, but didn't make it as a regular. He threw the discus as a member of the track team. Romare put down his discus when a baseball came onto the track, and threw the ball to home plate from beyond the outfield. So he was asked to join the school's baseball team.

He preferred the improvised games on sandlots, where they could play serious ball, and carouse after the game.

The girls who worked in the bakery next to the huge lot where Romare played baseball in the evenings would throw down cakes. "Or we'd leave school and go to the movies—I think it was eleven cents. A lot of the kids had secondhand Fords, painted all up, and drove to school. And so it was a lot of fun, football in the fall, going to basketball games in winter, and baseball in spring and summer."

Romare showed a talent for art by winning two poster contests. He won with the help of his grandmother, who taught him to simplify. The steel industry produced so much pollution that Pittsburgh was known as "Smoky City." The white shirt Romare put on for school in the morning was gray with soot by afternoon. So a poster contest was held for a citywide cleanup campaign. Romare went to the library to research his subject thoroughly—a lifelong habit—and started making sketches of Bessemer converters and open-hearth furnaces. Miss Carrie suggested that Romare simply "make it Mrs. McCarthy." She was a neighbor who chased Romare and his friends off her marble stoop with a broom, and, if they left even a scrap of litter, ordered them back to "Pick it up!" Romare got Mrs. McCarthy to model for him with her broom, captioned the poster "Pick It Up!" and won.

Gangster Gives Bearden a College "Scholarship"

Bearden's first benefactor was a Pittsburgh gangster named Mr. Druett. He distributed electrical refrigerator systems when most people still had "ice boxes," and the iceman went around the streets shouting "Ice!" Druett also had a "franchise" or concession with Brunswick records, which he delivered to various record stores around the city. He delivered more than records, however. Druett ran bootleg whiskey from Canada and sold it at a nightclub on a lake. He gave Romare a job at his establishment. Bearden knew about Druett's whiskey-running, but more he did not need or want to know. Romare worked for Druett one memorable summer near graduation from high school.

Druett was a contradictory and puzzling character. Even though he knew Romare was African-American, light-skinned as he was, he would hold the Indiana-based newspaper of the Ku Klux Klan in front of Romare's face and say, "This is America, boy; this is the real thing here—real America!" He was as vengeful toward people who crossed him as he was generous toward those he considered loyal. In short, Druett was a Pittsburgh version of a mobster in an era marked by racketeers.

Romare helped wash and wax Druett's cars. Another of his jobs was to supply Druett's wife, who loved chocolate, with her favorite candies. "She didn't like a bar of chocolate," Bearden remembered. "She liked *boxes.*" At the time, fifty cents bought a lot of candy, and for a dollar you could get a big box of chocolates or a pound of caramels. Romare would go around to various candy stores in search of the very best for Mrs. Druett, who would sit in the back of the automobile and eat candy all day. The relationship ended when Mrs. Druett got tired of popping sweets. One day, Romare saw her running naked down the street with Druett in pursuit. "I give you everything and how do you thank me?" he shouted. Evidently, she had entertained another man in Druett's absence and was sent away, unforgiven.

Above the garage, on the packed second floor of the house, Friday nights were devoted to "smoker movies"—the silent pornographic "flickers" of the time. Druett did not attend. He had little taste for art, either in film or on the canvas. When

Romare showed him one of the prizewinning posters he had done, Druett thought it was all right, but that the greatest artist in the world was Budd Fisher, who drew a comic strip called "Mutt and Jeff."

When Druett offered Romare the job at his nightclub, Romare's grandmother, unaware of the character of the place, voiced no objection. And at first it seemed harmless enough. Around the end of May, before the full season began, Romare would be driven to the resort, rent out canoes until 5 P.M., and be driven home. During the regular summer season, he stayed all weekend.

"He'd come and take me on Friday, and I would go out there and stay. They sold whiskey. Of course, this was during Prohibition, but he was in this group that ran name-brand whiskey in from Canada. Once they asked me if I wanted to go to Canada to make the whiskey run, but I said no."

Romare's job was to stand at the cash register at the back of the nightclub, where the waiters picked up ice, soft drinks, and whiskey. Druett trusted Romare and he was so young and innocent looking that he was the natural, designated holder of the big money. When the customers paid the waiters, they gave the money to Romare. Druett had told Romare to put anything over 200 dollars in his pocket instead of in the cash register.

Druett's relationship with the police, who were bribed regularly, was typical of the Prohibition era. "The motorcycle police would always come and knock on the window around ten-thirty or eleven at night, and they'd give them their drink through the window."

One weekend night, when Druett was away, a scene took place that might have come straight out of a gangster movie. "This man came in, I remember, in the summer heat with a derby hat on and asked to make a reservation for six. When they said yes, he said the cars would be right there. When they came back, the men had pistols and shotguns. Everybody had to get out of their seats and get up against the wall. Then they took the women's jewelry; they were fainting and screaming. They took the men's money, watches, and their rings had to come off.

"And then they came to me. It was 'Hands up!' Then the man looked at me and said, 'Put your hands down, kid. How much is in that thing?'" Romare gave him the 200 dollar limit from the till. "Then he said, 'Gee, ain't doin' no business tonight?' I was scared of getting shot or something, to tell him my pockets were down here with the money. So he took what was in the register and said, 'Give me a few bottles of whiskey.' He put the bottles in his pockets, and a couple in his hands, and then they left."

During all this, Romare heard the sputtering growl of the motorcycles and knew it was the cops. But there was no knocking at the window until after the mobsters had left. "I guess the cops looked in and saw what was happening, because two or three minutes after they were gone, the police came up and said, 'What's happened here?' Druett was there, so they called him, and he came. He asked what they looked like, but the police couldn't help, so Mr. Druett thanked them. They left, and then he took care of it himself. He made certain calls, asked 'And what did they look like?' and then said, 'Oh, these are guys from Detroit.' And I think about a week later, he made calls to Detroit, Cleveland, to know who they were. And they took care of the whole thing themselves. I don't know all the details—I didn't *want* to get into that."

When Romare handed Druett all the money he had been holding in his pockets, the mobster was overcome with gratitude. "And you know? He gave me enough for my first year in college! I left him to go to school. I left Pittsburgh."

College Days

Following high school graduation in 1929, Romare attended Lincoln University, a black, all-male university in Pennsylvania with a strong emphasis on academics. He soon transferred to Boston University, where he had friends and more choice of courses. During his two years at Boston, his artistic and athletic talents were in evidence. He was a star pitcher for the varsity team and pitched two summers for the Boston Tigers, a Negro team that played semi-pro exhibition games against other Negro teams like the Pittsburgh Crawfords and the Kansas City Monarchs.

Bearden was such a good pitcher that Connie Mack, owner of the Philadelphia Athletics, offered him a major-league contract if he would "pass" for white. Bearden was so light-skinned that he could have possibly done so, but he refused the offer. He saw no future for himself in the game as things then stood for Negro players, and he was becoming more and more interested in drawing.

"I had done some cartoons for the Boston University *Beanpot* but I wanted to be in New York." So in 1932 Bearden left baseball and Boston University, transferring to New York University (NYU). Back home in the family apartment in Harlem, he took the subway to classes in Washington Square.

As an undergraduate at NYU, Bearden's love of sciences and his talent for cartooning blossomed. He majored in mathematics, and drew regularly for the New York University *Medley*, a humor magazine with lots of drawings and editorial cartoons. Eventually, he became art editor. His best cartoon appeared after he graduated in June 1935. Bearden's cover drawing depicted a smiling bespectacled mathematics professor reading from his notes to a class of sleeping students. The cartoon said a lot about Romare: while he had a natural talent for mathematics, he loved art.

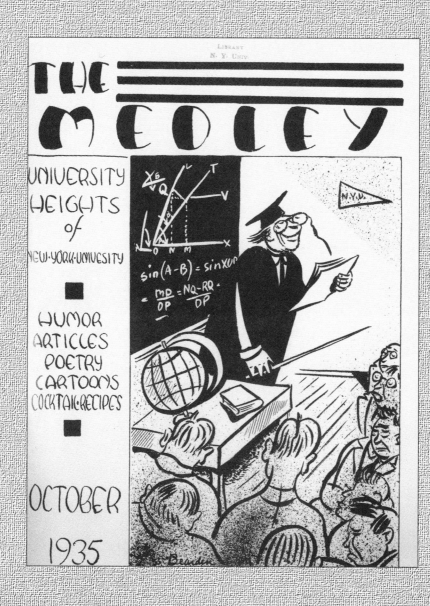

Romare Bearden's cover drawing for the October 1935 issue of the New York University Medley

This fact was a disappointment to his mother Bessye, who wanted her son to use his mathematics degree as a stepping stone to medical school. Bessye Bearden was a strong, outgoing woman, prominent in Harlem Democratic politics. She was also the New York editor of the most influential black newspaper in America, the *Chicago Defender*, and an adjuster for the Internal Revenue Service. She was called on to help resolve complicated and delicate tax matters. It must have been hard for Romare to summon up the courage to tell her that he wanted to be an artist.

Bearden had become friends with Elmer Simms Campbell, the first black cartoonist to be regularly published in the major magazines and make a good living as an illustrator. With Campbell's help, Bearden got his cartoons published in some of the big magazines, including *Life* and *Collier's*.

About a year after graduation, Bearden took Campbell's advice and became a student at the Art Students League. He studied in 1936–1937 with George Grosz, a gifted political cartoonist and master draftsman. His caricatures had made him the enemy of the emerging Nazi movement and forced him to flee Germany. Grosz's great book of drawings and watercolors, *Ecce Homo*, exposed the morally corrupt side of German life at the end of World War I. He portrayed the politicians, the military, and the capitalists as thugs, murderers, and gangsters who made their fortunes by exploiting the poor.

At the Art Students League, Grosz introduced Bearden to such master draftsmen of the past as Ingres, Hans Holbein, and Dürer. Romare's interest in cartooning led him to study the work of other great political satirists such as Honoré Daumier. Bearden was so interested in the work of Peter Brueghel that his friends at the League called him "Pete." But Grosz's most important lesson was teaching Bearden how to draw freely but with control. "Unlike the other students who usually were very tight I would draw all over the paper. And Grosz said, 'Now look, I want you to just draw the model's hand, or maybe just the face. Just use the whole paper and draw it here because I want you to really observe.' And this is what I did."

The Beardens had moved into a third-floor brownstone apartment on 131st Street between Seventh and Lenox Avenues. It was the choicest spot on the block. Bessye Bearden's parlor was a gathering spot for celebrities from many worlds—politics, journalism, show business, and the arts. The pianist-composers Fats Waller and Duke Ellington were family friends who later bought Bearden's early paintings. The apartment was usually full of relatives, friends, and about a dozen Siamese cats. (Like his mother, Romare loved cats, though he never had more than three.) Bessye could deal with almost anything. But once, when Romare's father was at his job as an inspector for the New York City Health Department, Romare came home to find his mother in bed, crying. "I said, 'What's the matter? You're sick.' She replied 'No, I'm by myself!'"

From their front window, Romare could see a passageway that led straight to the backstage entrance of Harlem's famous Lafayette Theater. The theater was a large building around the corner on Seventh Avenue between 131st and 132nd Streets. Near the Lafayette stood the Tree of Hope where all the performers gathered in the evening. Entertainers who were out of work would touch the tree for luck. Nearby was the downstairs entrance to Connie's Inn, where great black performers such as Duke Ellington and his Orchestra played to an all-white crowd.

A Studio of His Own

In 1935, the year he graduated from NYU, Bearden attended a meeting of some forty-five black artists at the 135th Street

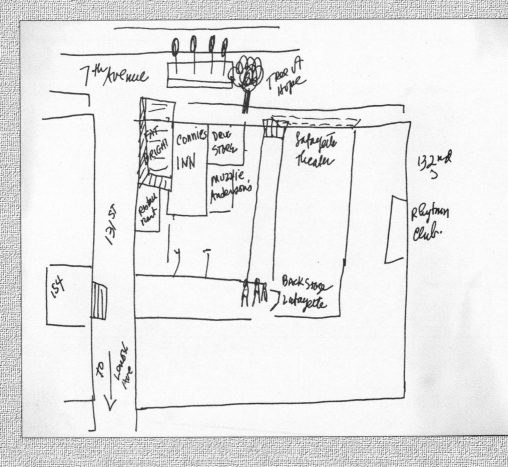

Bearden's sketch of his vibrant Harlem neighborhood in the 1930s. The Beardens' apartment at 154 West 131st Street was located across from the Lafayette Theater's backstage entrance and down the street from Connie's Inn and the Tree of Hope, where out-of-work entertainers congregated in the evenings.

YMCA. Looking around, Bearden was amazed to see so many black artists who were serious about organizing. The meeting marked the beginning of the Harlem Artists Guild, headed by the influential sculptor and teacher Augusta Savage.

That year, in the midst of the Great Depression, with over 13 million people unemployed, the administration of President Franklin Delano Roosevelt created the Works Progress Administration (WPA)/Federal Arts Project (FAP) to employ artists, writers, and theater people. The Harlem Artists Guild wanted the government to enroll more black artists in the WPA/FAP. Its efforts were successful. In 1937, with Eleanor Roosevelt attending the ceremonies, Augusta Savage was named director of the Harlem Community Art Center. It was housed in a loft at Lenox Avenue and 125th Street with 8,000 square feet (744 sq m) of studio space.

At another Harlem address, 306 West 141st Street, better known as "306," an informal group of black and white artists, writers, musicians, and theater people gathered at the studio of Bearden's cousin, the painter and teacher Charles "Spinky" Alston. Among the regulars were artists Augusta Savage and Aaron Douglas, as well as younger artists Jacob Lawrence and Gwendolyn Knight (who would later marry Lawrence), and Bearden, his school friend Norman Lewis, and the printmaker Robert Blackburn. The poets and novelists included Langston Hughes, Countee Cullen, Claude McKay, Gwendolyn Bennett, Alain Locke, Richard Wright, and Ralph Ellison. Ad Bates, a master cabinetmaker, dancer, and model for the Art Students League, lived there, along with Spinky and Henry Bannarn, a sculptor.

Artists were enrolled as either easel or mural painters under the WPA/FAP program. The Harlem Art Workshop was first located at the 135th Street Public Library. Then it moved to 306 with inexpensive studio, teaching, and living areas funded with

Members of the "306" group, including Charles Alston (in white shirt, center), Ad Bates (standing, far left), and Gwendolyn Knight (kneeling, far left), in front of 306 West 141st Street, in the mid-1930s

government money. Since Charles Alston was Harlem director of the WPA mural project, the artists came to 306 to report to him. It was an extraordinary social and artistic experiment that allowed artists to work and make a living. They created thousands of murals in hospitals, post offices, schools, and libraries.

Although Bearden was part of 306, his family income was too high for him to qualify as a WPA artist. In 1938, he became a full-time caseworker for the New York City Welfare Department, assigned to the men's division of the Harlem office. He held the job for three decades. In 1967, when an exhibition of his collages sold out, he retired. But his day job had lots of consequences. It disqualified him for WPA/FAP work, forced him to "moonlight" as an artist in the afternoons and evenings, and gave him an independent income, which enabled him to have his own studio over the years. It also made it impossible for him to combine painting with university teaching, which many of his friends eventually did, and exposed him to the trials of New York City's welfare population, who made up his caseload for many years.

In 1940, Bearden's friend Jacob Lawrence found him his first studio just west of Fifth Avenue on 125th Street. Bearden's studio was above Lawrence's. The rent was eight dollars a month, including electricity. His knew his other neighbors, writers Claude McKay and Bill Attaway and printmaker Bob Blackburn, from 306. What Romare didn't know was *what* to paint. The brown kraft paper (like the paper used in grocery bags) stood blank on his easel week after week.

One evening, walking downstairs with Claude, Romare heard the sound of keys jangling out in the street. It was a prostitute, as short and homely a woman as Bearden had ever seen. She said:

> "Two dollars, boys." Then she said "A dollar?" Then "Fifty cents?" Then, "A quarter?" Finally, she said "For God's sake, just take me." She was pathetic. I

told my mother about her, said she was in the wrong business, and my mother got a job for this woman—Ida. After that, Ida came every Saturday to clean my studio. And in the studio was my easel, with the piece of brown paper on it. When you're young, you have a lot of ideas and a lot of dreams, but you don't have the ability to realize them; I think that as you mature you don't have the same kind of ideas and dreams, because you let the work make its own fantasy. Anyway, Ida would come once a week to clean, and the brown paper was there on the easel, and one day she asked if it was the same piece of paper, and I told her that it was—that I didn't have my ideas together. She said, "Why don't you paint me?" Well, the way I must have looked at her she must have known what was going through my mind. "I know what I look like," she said. "But when you look and can find what's beautiful in me, then you're going to be able to do something on that paper of yours."

It was an important lesson for Romare. It taught him how to search for subject matter that was real to him.

That same year, during the first week in May, Ad Bates gave Bearden his first one-man show at 306. It consisted of work from his years at the Art Students League and after. While it was beautiful, it was not yet really his own; it was more the work a student does in studying the masters who came before him.

When the cold winter winds hit New York and Romare's landlord began to sell the radiators for scrap iron, it became unbearable in the studio. There was Romare, trying to paint with a stiff neck and colds hitting him in the muscles and joints.

Early in 1941, his mother helped him get a studio in the Apollo Guild right next to the Apollo Theater building at fifteen dollars a month. Now he was surrounded by musicians, composers, and his friends—the artist/photographers Morgan and Marvin Smith.

His friends Bill Attaway and Claude McKay gave him good advice: "Why don't you draw—you know, just let yourself go and draw some of the things you know about?" So Bearden began to do what he called his "Southern themes, the people that I'd seen as a young boy when I'd sometimes visit in North Carolina where I was born." He completed about twenty of these works, including *The Visitation* and *Folk Musicians* during the next year, 1941–1942.

The Visitation is done in dark, earthy tones—browns, reds, and greens. It shows two black women. Their faces are huge, showing that Bearden had looked closely at the work of the Mexican muralists Diego Rivera and José Orozco. The woman on the left is seen against a background of bare, black trees, rock, and hills. But next to the woman on the right, the gigantic leaves of a plant reach out toward the sky. The visitation will help her to flower. It was also the first flowering of Bearden's art.

5

Early Success

It was now early December 1941. Bearden, Jacob Lawrence, and other upcoming young black artists were about to exhibit their work. Two of Bearden's paintings, *The Bridge* (1937) and *After Church* (1941) were part of a major show of American Negro Art at the Downtown Gallery in midtown Manhattan. The day before the show opened, however, Japan launched a surprise attack on the U.S. fleet in Pearl Harbor, a vast sea and air base in Hawaii. As a result, the United States declared war on Japan. Bearden's debut would have to wait.

About three months later, Bearden enlisted in the all-black 372nd Infantry Division of the U.S. Army, which had a proud military history. Bearden's entire tour of duty, though, was spent in the United States. That allowed him to be near his studio and continue painting, at least during his first year of service.

During his World War II years, Romare saw his mother for the last time when he visited her in Harlem Hospital. When a telephone call came from his Aunt Clara on September 16, 1943, Romare steeled himself for the news. Bessye Bearden had died. Romare was thirty-two years old, and he had never had the chance to show his mother that he could truly make his mark on the world as an artist. As an only child, he had experienced all the privileges and turmoil that go along with an extraordinary woman's dreams. Bessye had taught him always to be concerned about others and never to tolerate injustice. She had also taught him the art of diplomacy, how to get along with people, without compromising his inmost beliefs.

Throughout the war, Bearden had been able to keep his studio next to the Apollo Theater in Harlem. During a leave in late 1943 or very early 1944, the painter William H. Johnson visited him there, bringing a well-known guest—Caresse Crosby. She was the widow of Harry Crosby and copublisher of the Black Sun Press in 1920s' Paris. She and her husband had known and published the early work of talented young Americans living in Paris, such as Ernest Hemingway, T. S. Eliot, F. Scott Fitzgerald, and John Dos Passos. After her husband's death, Caresse had helped save the lives and work of many French artists from the Nazis. Now she had opened a gallery of her own called G Place in Washington, D.C., and was particularly interested in the work of African-American painters. She decided that she wanted a show of Bearden's work.

In February 1944, Caresse Crosby gave Bearden a one-artist exhibition at her new gallery. And in June 1945, a month after Bearden's discharge from the army, Caresse gave him another one-artist show of watercolors and oil paintings called "The Passion of Christ." This exhibition, critically successful, was important for Bearden. To his Social Realist drawings and cartoons and his mural-influenced oils on Southern themes, he now added his own vision of the religious and literary subjects that had absorbed artists for centuries.

While Bearden's "The Passion of Christ" was still on the minds of the Washington art world, Caresse Crosby introduced Bearden to Samuel M. Kootz in New York. Kootz, about to open his own gallery, was ready to show the work of a new generation of young artists, which included Alexander Calder, Robert Motherwell, William Baziotes, Byron Browne, and Carl Holty. Bearden brought Kootz some watercolors, and he asked to see some oils also. Bearden had no oils ready, but now painted some on masonite board. Black linear outlines dominated the strong blues, yellows, oranges, reds, and purples.

Kootz liked the work so much that he wanted to give Bearden a show immediately. *The Passion of Christ* series, along with eleven new watercolors and eleven oils, was shown at the Kootz Gallery in October 1945. The show was a great success with the critics and public alike. Four days after it opened, seven oils and ten watercolors had been sold. Among the purchasers were Duke Ellington and the Museum of Modern Art. The museum's acquisition of the watercolor *He Is Arisen* was the first work of Bearden's purchased by a museum—and one of the world's leading museums at that.

Literature on the Easel

Early the next year, Bearden began work on another series of watercolors and oil paintings, all inspired by a poem "Lament for a Bullfighter, Ignacio Sanchez Mejias," about the ritual of heroism and death in the bullring by the famous Spanish poet, Federico García Lorca. The titles of Bearden's paintings were drawn from the mournful repetition of some of the poem's most famous lines, such as "At five in the afternoon."

In December 1946, Bearden's art took a lighter turn when he contributed several watercolors and oils to a group show called "Homage to Jazz." Ben Wolf, a reviewer for *Art Digest*, singled out

Romare Bearden (left) and Carl Holty (center) with Spanish painter Joan Miró during a visit to Holty's studio in 1948

Bearden's oil, *A Blue Note*, as "of particular interest compositionally, with its creation of a circular movement within a rectangle." Earlier, he had called one of Bearden's bullfight pieces "ambitious" in its understanding of form "that has little fear of large areas—a fortunate ability that should recommend him as a muralist." Now, in *A Blue Note*, Bearden had filled the space with the blues man holding a violin the size of a viola and about to bow his blue note. The critic's comment was an accurate prediction, as Bearden's later murals—about the times before the dawn and the "quilting bees" in Charlotte, jazzy evenings in Baltimore, and the history of Pittsburgh—adorned libraries, museums, and even subways in the cities where growing up had been a voyage of discovery.

Bearden's one-artist show for 1947 at the Kootz Gallery was again lighthearted, inspired by one of the great comic works of world literature, Rabelais's *Gargantua and Pantagruel*. Gargantua and Pantagruel are both giants in France with gargantuan appetites for overeating and drinking. (*Gar-gan-tu-a* means "What a large throat you have!" in medieval French.) The titles and subjects of Bearden's pieces were drawn from Rabelais: *Some Drink! Some Drink!* and *The Soul Never Dwells in a Dry Place*.

In July 1948, Kootz closed his gallery. He reopened it in 1949 but without Bearden, Carl Holty, and Byron Browne, whose work had easily recognizable human subject matter. Kootz had decided that the new direction in art—and sales—lay in the work of the abstract expressionists. These artists, mostly European émigrés to America, shared the idea that feeling, expressed through form and color, was the most important element in painting.

Bearden did his best work in watercolor in 1948–1949, after leaving the Kootz Gallery. In a one-artist exhibition at a small downtown gallery, he showed sixteen "variations" on the Greek poet Homer's great epic poem *The Iliad*. Bearden's imagination

This circa-1946 oil painting, A Blue Note, *is an early example of Romare Bearden's interest in jazz and improvisation. Its whereabouts are unknown.*

had been captured by Homer's classic retelling of the story of the Trojan War. These works were truly variations, like musical variations on a theme. Bearden's watercolors were delicate, often allowing the white of the paper to show through like light. He outlined the figures in variously colored inks, giving them the effect of the lead in stained-glass windows, like those of France's world-famous Chartres Cathedral. Bearden had studied reproductions of these windows at the Art Students League.

Although his *Iliad* show was well reviewed, Bearden missed being part of a group. He especially missed his friend Carl Holty, who had left New York for a teaching post at the University of Georgia. Now Bearden and Holty, a great theoretician with a thorough grounding in art history, began a year-long exchange of letters. Holty was especially good at explaining how Pablo Picasso, Georges Braque, and Juan Gris achieved their effects, and where they fell short. So a decade after his study with George Grosz, Bearden learned from Holty how to analyze the cubists. Holty also taught Bearden the importance of Henri Matisse and Piet Mondrian in their color, structure, and space.

Holty's most important advice, though, was that his young friend and student should leave the safe, familiar New York art scene. "What you need is banquet after banquet for your eyes. You are what you are but one has to be more than oneself."

Paris: A Banquet for the Eyes

Taking Holty's advice, Bearden applied as a graduate student at the Sorbonne University in Paris and was accepted. Since he was still eligible as a World War II veteran for benefits under the GI Bill of Rights, Bearden could receive seventy-five dollars monthly (about twice a French worker's monthly wage at the time) for tuition, art supplies, and room and board. He sailed for France early in 1950. Samuel Kootz had given him letters of introduction to Pablo Picasso, Georges Braque, Henri Matisse, and the abstract sculptor Constantin Brancusi. Carl Holty gave him letters to the painters Jean Hélion and Hans Reichel.

For Romare, Paris proved to be a "thing of dreams," a city built on a truly human scale. Although he knew that Manhattan's skyscrapers dwarfed Notre-Dame Cathedral, its main tower—a symbol of the finger of God pointing to the heavens—was awesome to Bearden. Because it was built in harmony with human measure, he wrote, "It seemed the most immense structure on earth."

In his furnished room on the Left Bank of the Seine, the traditional home of artists, Bearden had a skylit studio, ample heat, laundry, and three plentiful meals daily, all for forty dollars a month. At first, the freedom was a bit scary and left him feeling lost. Formal attendance at Sorbonne classes was not required. Strangely enough, though he bought an easel, brushes, and paints, he did not paint during his nine-month stay. He wrote Holty, "I just can't get my thoughts together yet. I recall that I used to be a painter back in the States, but I'll have to think about what I painted like." To his cousin Charles Alston, he wrote that in the great freedom of Paris, there was a danger that was hard to pin down: "You can sit at a café, no one bothers you, it's hard to find a waiter even to pay your bill—no one would say 'You lazy bastard, why don't you paint a picture, or write a poem.'"

Once he got accustomed to the lack of tension and the feeling that he needed to prove himself constantly as an artist, Bearden began to love Paris. He had sailed over with black friends from New York—the poet Myron O'Higgens and the photographer Marvin Smith, who had a *pension* in his building. In Paris he also met his friend, the painter Herbert Gentry. Like Bearden, Gentry had lived and painted in 1930s Harlem. But after serving in the army, Gentry had decided to study and live in Paris, and had opened the Club Galérie, an art salon by day and a jazz club by night, drawing an international crowd of artists and intellectuals.

Of James Baldwin, Richard Wright, and Albert Murray

Holty had been right. Paris was a world so saturated with artistic and intellectual excitement that it would surely force Bearden "to become more than himself." The reason Bearden did not paint during his stay probably lay in the city's very exuberance. The "banquet after banquet for the eyes" was simply too much for Bearden to digest so quickly. Richard Wright had become a French citizen, James Baldwin read from his new novel, *Go Tell It on the Mountain,* and the great clarinetist and soprano saxophonist Sydney Bechet was playing in the clubs. With old friends like Herbert Gentry, and new friends like the novelist and critic Albert Murray, Bearden went to all the museums. He walked in the beautiful parks, the Luxembourg Gardens and the Tuileries Gardens near the Louvre, one of the world's great museums. He took in everything, swimming like a fish in water with its mouth wide open.

Once, sitting at the Dôme Café on Boulevard Montparnasse, Bearden felt the crowd getting excited. A waiter hollered something like "He is passing by!" It was Henri Matisse, the great modernist master, supported by a young man and a young woman. People started clapping. Matisse didn't pay attention until the young man said, "That applause is for you." Matisse was delighted and started to smile. All the people were reaching over to shake hands with him. Romare thought, "Isn't this wonderful! They're not applauding a movie star, but a man who changed the way we see life because he is a great painter." That was what made Paris magic for Bearden.

The day before he sailed back to New York, Bearden dashed around Paris in a last-minute search for art supplies, buying different colors and thicknesses of rice paper. It would be years before he used them, or applied the theories he had worked out with Holty. When he did, it renewed his art. But on that last Paris day in very late summer, Bearden's friend Albert Murray remembered Romare's eyes getting more and more moist the later it got.

6

Uptown Manhattan Skyline: Storm Approaching

Back in New York City in his old studio next to the Apollo Theater in 1951, Romare was not painting regularly. Instead, he paced back and forth, smoking cigarettes to calm his nerves, and dreaming about going back to Paris. His GI benefits had run out, and there seemed to be no way of raising the money to return. Romare stared at the upright piano in his studio, all that was left of an old rehearsal hall. He was struck with an idea, perhaps born of a desperate need to be back in Paris, and happy once again.

Romare approached old friends who made their living in music: Dave Ellis, a composer and arranger; Joshua Lee and Frank Fields, black classical composers; and Fred Norman, a successful black composer of pop songs. "Teach me how to write a song here; I've heard of Irving Berlin and these people who made a lot of money on one hit song."

Bearden made no headway with songwriting until he met Laertes (Larry) Douglas, a publicity man. One day, while

Miss Bertha and Mr. Seth
1978
Collage
25 ½ x 18 ½ in.
(65 x 47 cm)

They rented a house from my grandfather.

I can still smell the flowers she used to
give us and still taste the blackberries.

Maudell Sleet's Magic Garden
1978
Collage on board
10 ⅛ x 7 in.
(26 x 18 cm)

Sunset and Moonrise with Maudell Sleet
1978
Collage
41 x 29 in.
(104 x 74 cm)

When her husband died she worked the farm, most of the time by herself.

The last time I saw Liza was down at the station when I left for Pittsburgh on the 5:13.

Sunset Limited
1978
Collage
15 ½ x 20 ¼ in.
(39 x 52 cm)

Mill Hand's Lunch Bucket
1978
Collage
13¾ x 18⅛ in.
(35 x 46 cm)

The mills went 24 hours a day with three 8-hour shifts.

Early Carolina Morning
1978
Collage
29 x 41 in.
(74 x 104 cm)

67

Guitar Executive
1979
Collage
9 x 6 in.
(23 x 15 cm)

Pittsburgh Memory
1964
Photomontage
27½ x 35⅞ in.
(70 x 91 cm)

Farewell Eugene
1978
Collage
16 ¼ x 20 ½ in.
(41 x 52 cm)

At Connie's Inn
1974
Collage with acrylic and lacquer
50 x 40 in.
(127 x 102 cm)

The Visitation
1941
Tempera on composition board
30 x 46 in.
(76 x 117 cm)

He Is Arisen
1945
Black and colored ink on paper
26 x 19⅜ in.
(66 x 49 cm)

Pablo Picasso

Violin, Bottle and Glass
1913
Oil, collage and charcoal on canvas
25½ x 20 in.
(65 x 50 cm)

Stuart Davis

Egg Beater No. 1
1927
Oil on canvas
29⅛ x 36 in.
(74 x 91 cm)

A Walk in Paradise Gardens
1955
Oil on masonite
33½ x 29¼ in.
(85 x 74 cm)

Bearden was painting, there was a knock on his door. It was Larry. "Open the window!" he commanded Bearden. "That's my song they're playing." A tune was blaring across 125th Street from the outdoor speaker of a record shop.

Over the next couple of years, Bearden published about twenty tunes with Larry Douglas and Fred Norman. The most famous was a sensual Latin beguine called "Seabreeze" (which a liquor company used to promote a drink of the same name). It was recorded by the singer Billy Eckstein, the great jazz cellist Oscar Pettiford, and later by Tito Puente. But it didn't get him back to Paris.

The new movement in the New York art world was abstract expressionism. As far as this trend was concerned, Bearden felt that it was not the way he wanted to paint. "Nor do I feel that one should put up a predetermined set of rules about what to do or not do in painting. I did try some experiments with Carl Holty in the use of color—that it sometimes broke open the picture for me—that it seemed to run away and not stay on the canvas. So I just began to work in bigger chords of color that turned out to look like an oriental carpet of some kind. Then just as color was getting away from me, so did painting as a whole."

At the same time, Bearden knew that he was not really cut out to be a songwriter. He was only partly aware of the psychological storm headed his way. European friends, the essayist and philosopher Hannah Arendt and her husband, philosopher Heinrich Blucher, lived close to the Bearden family apartment near Columbia University. Hannah and Heinrich warned Romare not to get sidetracked with music. "If you keep on, you're going to ruin yourself as a painter, because you're just not attuned to this," Heinrich said. But Romare was feeling lost. One day he collapsed on the street, and woke up in the hospital. When he asked what had happened, a doctor said, "You blew a fuse." Romare had experienced a nervous breakdown.

He recovered quickly, and wrote Holty, "Now I'm going to do nothing but paint—no more wildcat schemes to get rich quick with a hit song. Creative work never leaves you with the kind of tension I had built up." He was ready for a new life and a renewed art.

At a benefit dance for victims of a West Indies hurricane, Romare met a quiet, smiling, lovely young woman named Nanette Rohan, whose parents came from French St. Martin in the Caribbean. They fell in love. Several months later, on September 4, 1954, two days after Romare's forty-third birthday, they were married.

In 1956, with Nanette's encouragement and the help of Merton Simpson, a friend who dealt in African art, the Beardens moved to a combination studio-apartment at 357 Canal Street. The fifth-floor walk-up loft was in an industrial area near several well-known New York neighborhoods: Greenwich Village, an artists' milieu reminiscent of Paris, and Chinatown, one of the largest concentrations of immigrants from China in the United States. Bearden's longtime friend from his schooldays, the painter Norman Lewis, had moved downtown from Harlem, and Carl Holty was back in New York.

Stuart Davis, American Cubism, and the Sweet Jazz of Life

The painter Stuart Davis lived in a studio-apartment nearby in Greenwich Village with his wife and son. He and Bearden had become close nearly ten years earlier. Davis was probably Bearden's most important influence. They shared many interests. Davis had been to Paris much earlier than Bearden, and had painted there. He loved sports, had watched world-champion black boxer Jack Johnson spar, and had gone with Holty and Bearden to baseball games. Other painters had known how important Stuart Davis was for decades—he had taken cubism and jazzed it up, reinventing it as an *American* art.

Cubism, the revolution in art launched by Pablo Picasso (see page 71) and George Braque in 1909, deliberately turned away from realistic representation of objects. Objects were broken apart in geometrical compositions on the flat surface of the picture.

In his famous *Egg Beater* series (see page 72), Davis showed how you could look at an egg beater "inside out," from all sides at once. For Bearden, Davis's paintings showed a way of getting right to the essence of what color could express about America and its unique art form—jazz. "His art has that kind of quality," Bearden said. "The lettering, jazz." Davis played records of the great jazz pianist Earl Hines by the hour, making Bearden listen for the syncopations, the use of space, and the intervals. ("The interval," he explained, "is what you leave out.") When Bearden brought his work for Davis to critique, he used jazz to make his point. If Bearden had too much regularity on each side of the painting, "Stuart used to say, 'You've got to look at varying things. Say you have people walking—you have to consider these things as musical beats.' Most people differentiate color and form. But for Stuart, these things were one: color, form—all of them affecting one another. He would always say, 'Color has a position and a place, and it makes space.'"

When Bearden returned fully to painting in the mid-1950s, he showed how well he'd gotten Davis's point. His oil painting of a procession, *A Walk in Paradise Gardens* (1955), used big tracks of color in a cubist manner so that each leg, each arm, each face, each body, was broken up into several different color planes. In *Mountains of the Moon* (1956) the tracks of color were blue, with heavily built-up layers. His one-artist exhibition, his first since 1949, had reviewers praising "a sea change in manner" with "heavily charged" color and "a new freedom in his space-filling figure paintings."

Chinese Landscape Painting

After moving to Canal Street, Bearden met Mr. Wu, a bookseller whose shop was on Bayard Street. Although Wu was not himself an artist, Bearden regarded him as a master teacher of Chinese art. He began to work with Wu on the spirit of Chinese painting—the perspective. "The great [Chinese] landscapes usually use three perspectives: the lower part as if you were looking down upon it; the middle part as if you were looking at it straight on from the front; the mountains at the top as if you were looking upward at them." Wu taught Bearden a new way of seeing the world. In Chinese landscape painting, from the secure situation of the philosopher or poet, one sees the world becoming *larger* as it recedes. This was opposite to the Renaissance perspective, the Western concept creating the illusion of things getting *smaller* as they recede in space. It was more in keeping with Bearden's liking for flatter space, "because it did away with illusionary space . . . and this allowed me to free myself."

From Wu, Bearden also learned about the "open corner" of Chinese landscape painting—usually the upper right-hand corner. It allows the viewer to enter the painting, completing areas the artist has purposely left unfinished. And, using an ancient Chinese method he had discussed with Wu, Bearden started to make a turn toward collage.

In the Western tradition, collage had been an outgrowth of cubism for Braque and Picasso. First they added words and numbers to their cubist compositions. Then in the spirit of modern life, they began to improvise with "found" objects taken from the real world: bits of actual newspaper, wallpaper, sheet music, or oilcloth. These were layered one on top of another to create new, often musical compositions with cutouts reminding the viewer of musicians, still lifes of bottles and fruits, or harlequins and other circus performers. Bearden began his collage work by using the classic techniques: *collage,* the cutting and pasting of *papier collé* (cut paper); *déchirage,* or tearing away; and applying large areas of color. With big brushes, Bearden painted broad areas of color on different thicknesses of rice paper, like those he'd searched for on his last day in Paris. He glued these to the canvas in as many as nine layers. Then he tore sections of the paper away, always tearing upward and across. When he found a pattern he liked, he added more papers and more color to complete the work.

Then, still under Wu's guidance, Bearden started to paint in oils that had the delicate thinness of watercolor, as if the light could shine through. "I would paint, then take turpentine and wash it out, so a few stains would remain; then I'd paint again." Now, after years of study with Wu, Bearden was emphasizing pure *feeling* in his art, and had found what the greatest artists seek: the ability to take chances, to surprise yourself, to combine the spontaneous freedom of a child with the experience of a master. As early as 1961, Bearden created a collage called *Circus,* cutting acrobats from prepared paper and placing them on a bicycle or walking a high wire on top of funny tenement roofs. Here he was at fifty, a spiritual child of Picasso's and Braque's work in collage, playing with scissors, prepared paper, and glue.

In early 1960 and again in 1961, Bearden was given well-received one-artist exhibitions of the delicate abstractions that emerged from his years of study with Stuart Davis and Wu. He first showed at the Michel Warren Gallery, then at the Cordier-Warren Gallery. After that, and for the rest of his life, Bearden showed at the Cordier and Ekstrom Gallery.

Cordier and Ekstrom had its roots in the Parisian art world. Daniel Cordier, a hero of the French Resistance, had served as secretary to the legendary Resistance fighter Jean Moulin, who was discovered by the Nazis, tortured, and executed. Daniel Cordier barely survived the Nazi occupation himself. After the war, he opened a gallery. Arne Ekstrom and his wife Parmenia had met young Michel Warren in Paris. The Ekstroms helped to set Warren up with a New York gallery, and later, Warren convinced Cordier, owner of a now important Paris gallery, to form a business venture with Ekstrom.

For two years, the Warren-Ekstrom-Cordier association flourished, with Ekstrom as silent partner. On a cold November evening in 1959, Warren and Ekstrom knocked on the door of 357 Canal Street to see Bearden's work. "The stairs rose to the sky," Mr. Ekstrom recalled. They were met by Nanette, Romare, and Gyppo, their cat. "This cat *flung* itself from one painting to another, not tearing the canvas, but gripping the top." Despite the climb and his fear that Gyppo would destroy a canvas, Ekstrom liked Bearden's work immensely, as did Warren. So Bearden had his first shows. It was the first of many visits Ekstrom was to make to Bearden's studio.

The Cordier-Warren gallery was quite prestigious, showing the work of such well-known artists as Cordier's friends Jean Dubuffet and Henri Michaux, and the sculptor Matta. The gallery was able to add the work of sculptor Isamu Noguchi. Bearden was proud to join the group.

Meanwhile Michel Warren left the gallery and it became Cordier and Ekstrom. In 1964, Daniel Ekstrom closed his own Paris gallery in a much publicized letter. In it, Arne Ekstrom said, "he decided to tell the world his thoughts about galleries, the world of art, in fact the very status of painting and sculpture." Cordier thought things were changing for the worse. The

New York gallery name remained Cordier and Ekstrom as did the warm relationship, but the financial arrangement ended.

Civil Rights and the Spiral Group

Bearden's decisive leap into collage-making came as a result of his affiliation with a group of black artists called Spiral. With Bearden's old friend Norman Lewis as the group's first chairman, his cousin Charles Alston and his friend Hale Woodruff as founding members, and Bearden as secretary, the group first met at Bearden's Canal Street studio.

As the foreword to Spiral's 1965 show made clear, the group had come together in the summer of 1963, before the important Civil Rights march on Washington during which Dr. Martin Luther King, Jr., gave his famous speech to more than 100,000 people at the Abraham Lincoln Memorial. Dr. King's theme was brotherhood, and he repeated several eloquent phrases with the effect of biblical prophecy: "I have a dream!"; "Let freedom ring"; and "Free at last! Lord God Almighty, I'm free at last."

As far as the Spiral group was concerned, in answer to the question "Why are we here?" Hale Woodruff had answered: because "We, as Negroes, could not fail to be touched by the outrage of segregation, or fail to relate to the self-reliance, hope, and courage of those who were marching in the interest of man's dignity. . . . We hoped with our art to justify life."

Emma Amos, one of the group's younger members, remembers Bearden's collecting "an enormous picture file, all cut out in shapes and stuffed in a bag. He brought it to the Spiral meeting place on Christopher Street and spread it all out on the floor, suggesting we make a collaborative collage." Everybody but Bearden soon lost interest, so he went ahead on his own. Another Spiral friend, Reginald Gammon, suggested that Bearden take the five or six small photomontages he'd

This booklet cover for Spiral's 1965 group show was chosen because starting from a starry center, the spiral moves outward, embracing all directions.

done and enlarge them photostatically up to 3 by 4 feet (91 by 122 cm). Originally cut from both black-and-white and color photographic images and then layered, the enlargement process made them huge, and gave them a documentary, black-and-white quality.

Projections

When Arne Ekstrom came to Bearden's studio in spring 1964 to discuss a fall show, the enlargements were rolled up in a corner. "What are those?" he asked. Bearden dismissed them, saying they probably wouldn't be of interest, that their content was probably too strong. But Ekstrom was fascinated and asked Bearden if he could create another twenty over the summer. They could be exhibited as "Projections," suggesting the process as well as the strong photographic and documentary quality of the "montage paintings."

The projections were shown at Cordier and Ekstrom in October 1964 with their tiny "source collages," often 8½ by 11 inches (22 by 28 cm) and then at the Corcoran Gallery, an important museum in Washington, D.C., a year later. A 1964 letter written by Arne Ekstrom describes them well: "They are really extraordinary and constitute a sort of re-living and re-telling of his memories as a Negro. The subjects range from burials and cotton fields to jam sessions, Harlem streets, Conjur women, etc. In these days of civil rights strife they are, on the sociological side, a unique statement of pride in tradition, dramatic in many instances but never a form of protest or agitation. Artistically they are most remarkable."

The critics agreed. Charles Childs, writing in *Art News*, described how "subjects of a half-forgotten Negro world . . . will surprise many who thought they knew Bearden from his abstractions." Dore Ashton, writing in *Quadrum* (Brussels), likened

"Projections" to an indictment ("a piercing activist bill of particulars") of intolerable facts. The *New York Times* review called it "knockout work of its kind."

Bearden was back. He had arrived at long last, rediscovering himself as an artist once again, by reinventing collage as a uniquely American art form with African-American subject matter represented with such genius that it became universal.

7

Triumph and Recognition

One late spring day in 1971, a thirty-year retrospective of the art of Romare Bearden called "The Prevalence of Ritual"opened at New York City's Museum of Modern Art. For any artist, perhaps especially for an African-American, this was a long awaited moment. By then, Bearden had worked half his life to succeed, and a walk through this exhibition showed that he had lived up to the highest expectations. The show was a triumph.

For a viewer unfamiliar with Bearden's art, the pictures at this exhibition were a bit perplexing, since the works of various periods were so different from one another. The first group, from 1940 to 1942, for instance, was composed of large works painted in gouache on brown paper. They had titles like *Serenade, The Visitation*, and *Folk Musicians. The Visitation* was interesting: Bearden had taken a theme from the religious art of Europe going back hundreds of years—the visitation by an angel to announce to Mary that she would give birth to Jesus—

and transposed it to the South he remembered from his earliest youth.

Another of these works, *Folk Musicians,* was a realistic portrait of three men staring directly at the viewer, with the middle figure holding a guitar. It wasn't an attempt to capture a photographic likeness, though. The hands, especially those of the guitar player, are huge. The triangular noses of the two left figures are much larger than scale, and the interplay of caps, noses, and faces is a study in diagonals.

Further along in the exhibition was a huge work entitled *Three Folk Musicians* (1967). It bore a striking similarity to the earlier work in that it was again a study of three figures, each now holding a guitar or a banjo, seen full face looking at the viewer. In many ways, however, this work couldn't have been more different. In the 1967 version, pieces of photographs are mixed with cut and pasted paper and painted in brilliant color to create a collage. Bearden had reinvented the technique in order to transform his own early themes with striking contrasts of color and playfulness. Like its 1941 version, the 1967 work shows a musician at the right—now a banjo player whose rounded face resembles Bearden's own. The banjo player is made ghostly and mysterious by the blue-grays of his torso, the streaks of blue and white through his face, and his eyes, which have the stare of stone statuary. The white disk of his banjo echoes the red disk of the sun, and is set off by the warm yellows of the two guitars.

Other collages were named individually under the umbrella title *The Prevalence of Ritual.* These made up a group with such titles as *The Prevalence of Ritual: Conjur Woman as an Angel; The Prevalence of Ritual: Baptism;* and *The Prevalence of Ritual: Tidings.* It's important to notice that this group of collages had the same title as the entire exhibition. While the titles were lyric, spiritual, and religious, their overtones were a continuation of the Southern landscape of Bearden's early work.

Still other collages had been photo-enlarged from their original dimensions to large 6- by 8-foot (1.8- by 2.4-m) panels entitled *Projections*. In this way, Bearden had taken a small collage like *The Dove*, filled with people in a Harlem street (with the dove of the title perched in the collage's center, just above the arch of an apartment building's entrance), and photo-enlarged it to huge proportions. Another, *The Prevalence of Ritual: Baptism*, was filled with masklike figures wading in a stream's waters during a baptism. These intricately crafted collages in soft, pale colors became monumental when they were photo-enlarged.

Yet another group of at least twenty works, many of them created in 1967, had the huge, imposing quality of the 6- by 8-foot (1.8- by 2.4-m) *Projections*, but were themselves collages. Like *Three Folk Musicians*, they were filled with bright color. Their titles were lyrical, reminiscent of the stillness and quiet of Southern scenes.

Time of day, season, work, and place often rooted these works in such titles as *Early Morning, Evening Meal, Backyard, Summer Song, Summertime, Rites of Spring*, and *Melon Time*. These titles, written in collaboration with Albert Murray, reflected Bearden's awareness of the musical traditions—classical, popular, sacred, and secular—that made his art so sonorous and colorful. He, like his friend Albert Murray, had read the French poet Stéphane Mallarmé's famous poem *"L'Après Midi d'un Faune"* ("The Afternoon of a Faun"). (It had been danced in Paris early in the century by the world-famous Ballets Russes, with sets painted by Pablo Picasso and music composed by Igor Stravinsky.) At the same time, Bearden was familiar with Stravinsky's powerful *Rite of Spring*, as well as George

Gershwin's opera *Porgy and Bess,* which gave the song "Summertime" to the world. Later, Bearden would himself collaborate on backdrops and "scrims"—painted, luminous curtains—for the Alvin Ailey American Dance Theater.

He was even more aware of the tradition in art, and was singular among twentieth-century artists in drawing upon an astonishingly diverse multitude of cultures and traditions. He used African masks; Chinese landscape painting; Persian miniatures; Renaissance and Dutch masters, such as Breughel the Elder, Rembrandt, Reubens, Raphael, and Vermeer; and French impressionists and postimpressionists, such as Matisse, Cezanne, and Picasso. All of this transformed the everyday into the timeless: black subjects in the fields, in the garden, at the bath, in a stream at a baptism, playing folk guitars (such as the masterful *Guitar Executive*) or jazzy valve trombones.

Among the showstoppers of the exhibition were several large collages created in 1970: *She-Ba* (Solomon's African Queen), a work 4 by 3 feet (122 by 91 cm), showing Sheba in regal dress, wearing an ornate crown, escorted by an attendant holding an umbrella against the sun, and *Patchwork Quilt,* a collage 3 by 4 feet (91 by 122 cm), depicting a nude lying facedown, her left arm extended along her back and her head in profile, on a sofa topped by a patchwork quilt in a symphony of colors. Finally: *The Block,* a collage of six side-by-side panels, 4 by 18 feet (1.2 by 5.5 m) overall, showing a funeral; an Annunciation with black angels ascending the apartment wall above the funeral to heaven; and a group of storefronts at street level, including a liquor store, the Sunrise Baptist Church, and the Mirror Barber Shop. The brownstones in the work, their colors tracked vertically side-by-side, create the effect of a piano keyboard. The viewer took in the collage against a pre-recorded "tape collage" of street noise, church music, blues, laughing voices, and the sounds of children at play.

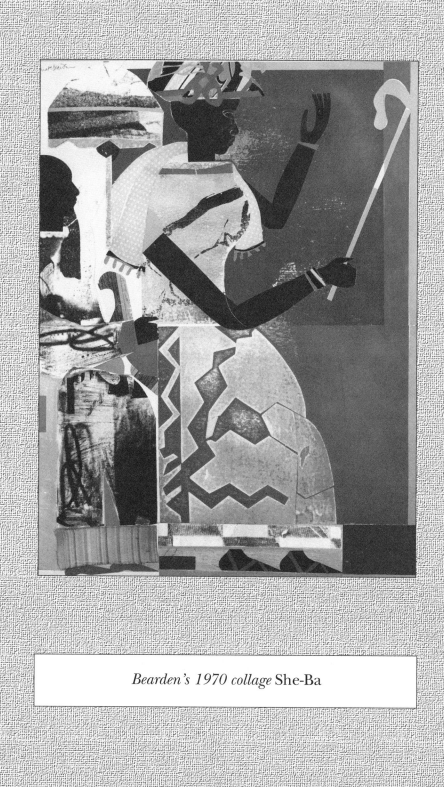

Bearden's 1970 collage She-Ba

In his art, Bearden was "trying to explore, in terms of the particulars of the life I know best, those things common to all cultures." Indeed, Bearden said, "Art celebrates a victory." He had searched for and found the elements in which life expresses that victory, even in the midst of an increasingly dehumanizing technological society. "The Prevalence of Ritual," wrote curator Carroll Greene, "is more than an exhibition; it is an affirmation, a celebration, a victory of the human spirit over all the forces that would oppress it." In fact, Bearden's art celebrated a victory over the very forces that gave rise to it.

Before the MoMA Exhibit

The success of Bearden's one-artist exhibit at the Museum of Modern Art (MoMA) in 1971 was no accident. Four years earlier, Bearden had already moved to large "in-your-face" collages, often 4 by 5 feet (1.2 by 1.5 m), was working in color, and showed increasing sensitivity for the properties of paper. Instead of using prepared paper, for instance, he painted the paper himself before pasting it down, first on composition board, then on hard masonite board, which solved a frustrating problem. Bearden had been stretching his canvases so tightly that the stretchers began to snap with the pressure. Finally, his friend Jack Schindler showed Bearden how to improve his technique of backing the canvas, and finally suggested that Bearden abandon canvas altogether in favor of masonite board. Schindler also suggested that Bearden rent a studio in an office building in Long Island City, an area that was just beginning to be used by artists as working space.

With this move, the rhythm of Bearden's life was renewed. He was living on Canal Street in Soho (the area South of Houston Street), which was then becoming popular among artists. He traveled on the elevated train to his studio in Long

Island City, known mostly for its industry, manufacturing, and low-priced office space. He could show up at his third-floor studio by 9:45 A.M. looking like a construction worker in his blue overalls (with the initials RB stitched over his chest), feed the pigeons that greeted him at his windows, and return home to Canal Street after a solid, five- or six-hour workday. In reality he was a construction worker—but his constructions would last longer than the buildings in which they were created.

Bearden's 1967 one-artist show at Cordier and Ekstrom sold out. (The last collage was purchased by New York Senator Jacob Javits for his wife Marion, who instructed her husband not to come home without it.) With this success, Bearden underwent another fundamental change. At age fifty-six, he was finally able to retire from the Department of Social Services and spent the next twenty years painting full-time.

Following his 1967 success at Cordier and Ekstrom by a week, the landmark exhibition "The Evolution of Afro-American Artists: 1800–1950" codirected by Bearden and Carroll Greene, Jr., opened at the Great Hall of City College of the City University of New York. The comprehensive exhibit brought together 120 paintings and sculptures by 53 Afro-American artists. Many of these artists had never been shown before in America, much less in Harlem, where Bearden had grown up and attended P.S. 5 on 135th Street, a short walk from the exhibit. It might be a short walk, but it had been a long journey.

In November 1968, Bearden's "Paintings and Projections" was installed at the Art Gallery of the State University of New York at Albany. To twenty-one of the 1964 black-and-white projections, Bearden added seven collages created between 1965 and 1968, executed on the same 4- by 3-foot (122- by 91-cm) scale but collaged with paper layered on paper in color. The smallest was *The*

Fiddler (1965), 30¾ by 24 inches (78 by 61 cm); the largest was *Circe Preparing a Banquet for Ulysses* (1968), 44 by 56 inches (112 by 142 cm). The catalog introduction by novelist Ralph Ellison (*Invisible Man*, 1947), much reprinted, remains among the most eloquent pieces ever written on Bearden's art. That essay—and Bearden's art—put the artist on America's cultural map.

Late in 1969, Romare Bearden, Norman Lewis, and Ernest Crichlow founded the Cinque Gallery, named after Joseph Cinque, the hero who led a rebellion aboard the slave ship *Amistad.* The three men had asked the Ford Foundation for seed money to start a nonprofit gallery that would serve as a showcase for young minority artists, including women, African-Americans, and Hispanic people, and provide art history majors with the chance to work as curators and gallery directors. "The Foundation had given 1 million dollars for the improvement of black businesses in Harlem. Why shouldn't the Ford Foundation do it?" they felt. The three friends then spent over half a year looking for a suitable location. They approached Joseph Papp, whose New York Public Theater space on Lafayette Street seemed ideal, and he was all for the idea. After the Ford Foundation gave Cinque a 30,000 dollar grant and Joe Papp made the space available, Cinque was born.

The Cinque Gallery was a demonstration of Bearden's life-long commitment to helping younger artists—in the public schools, and at such colleges as Williams and Bard, and at Howard University—to become teachers, artists, gallery directors, and museum curators.

8

Of the Blues

The blues and jazz have been intertwined with the art of the twentieth century since the arrival of the first American jazz bands in Europe after World War I. Igor Stravinsky, an important classical composer, called a piece he wrote early in the century *Ragtime*, a tribute to the way black pianists such as Scott Joplin took European harmonies and "ragged" them with left-hand syncopations. The incorporation of Afro-American jazz into the European classical repertoire changed the way audiences heard music. Pablo Picasso's two versions of *Three Masked Musicians* (1920), a landmark cubist work, melded Italian *commedia dell'arte* with its street harlequins and musical instruments, African sculpture, and New Orleans funeral parade music. Stuart Davis, who transformed cubism to make it purely American, used the piano recordings of Earl Hines for inspiration. George Gershwin, who lived in Paris during the 1920s, wrote the opera *Porgy and Bess*, and opened the jazz vocabulary to such compositions as "Summertime" and "Bess, You Is My

Woman Now." Henri Matisse entitled an entire series of his "cutouts" *Jazz* (1943–1944) and Piet Mondrian, intoxicated by the lights, rhythms, music, and energy of New York, painted *Broadway Boogie Woogie* (1942–1943).

Among artists of the twentieth century, Romare Bearden has been unique in capturing the celebratory essence of jazz and the blues in his art. He could remember E. C. Johnson's blues from the time he was ten years old summering with his Grandmother Cattie. Much later, Romare borrowed the title *Carolina Shout* from James P. Johnson, one of the great stride pianists and composers, for a large, powerful collage in a series entitled *Of the Blues*. Bearden's immersion in jazz filled his years as a young painter in Harlem.

The Meaning of the Blues

"As a young boy," Bearden told an interviewer, "I'd go to the Lafayette Theater in Harlem, and I'd hear Bessie Smith or some other singer. What they sang would usually go like this: 'I woke up this morning and my man left me a note. He said he was leaving, and I'm feeling so blue, so blue. I'm goin' down by the river and if I feel as bad as I do now, I'm gonna jump in.' Here she's talking about a poignant personal event—her love is gone. But behind her the musicians are 'riffing,' changing something tragic into something positive and farcical. This is why I've gone back to the South and to jazz. Even though you go through these terrible experiences, you come out feeling good. That's what the blues say and that's what I believe—life will prevail."

As Bearden wrote in 1987 for an exhibition of his jazz work entitled *Riffs and Takes*: "Some years ago, I showed a watercolor to Stuart Davis, and he pointed out that I had treated both the left and right sides of the painting in exactly the same way. After that, at Davis's suggestion, I listened for hours to recordings of

Earl Hines at the piano. Finally, I was able to concentrate on the silences between the notes. I found that this was very helpful to me in the transmutation of sound into colors and in the placement of objects in my paintings and collages. I could have studied this integration and spacing in Greek vase painting, among many examples, but with Earl Hines I ingested it within my own background. Jazz has shown me the ways of achieving artistic structures that are personal to me, but it also provides me continuing finger-snapping, head-shaking enjoyment of this unique, wonderful music."

The format of the nineteen-collage *Of the Blues* begins with the ancestral roots of the music and then follows it to a rural Mecklenburg County setting, both secular and sacred. Two funeral scenes again trace this sacred-secular transition in New Orleans. *New Orleans Farewell*, for instance, is a large 44- by 50-inch (112- by 127-cm) collage depicting the many mourners, including uniformed musicians with trumpets, trombone, and tuba, at the funeral itself. Then, in a complementary collage, the musicians parade back to a saloon to celebrate the departed with such "rags" as "Didn't He Ramble." *New Orleans Ragging Home* depicts just such a musical parade past onlookers in the balcony of what could very well be a bordello. The secular side of the music is nowhere more evident than in the *Storyville* collages like the small, exquisite *Storyville* showing a piano player in the foreground surrounded by odalisques. As Albert Murray points out, *Empress of the Blues* could be Ma Rainey, Bessie, Mamie, or Trixie Smith, or Ida Cox. The dapper musicians behind her, in their bow ties and slick threads, could as easily be in the band of Duke Ellington, or Chick Webb, or Fletcher Henderson.

The famous dance and jazz palaces are depicted in some of the most celebratory and powerful collages Bearden ever produced. These include *At Connie's Inn,* featuring an entire band swinging together before the footlights underneath the club's ornate curtain. *Wrapping It up at the Lafayette* is another show-stopping collage, this time focusing on the gigantic curtain that occupies the top half of the large 4- by 3-foot (122- by 91-cm) collage, with a blazing sun in the center of a "jungle" scene. A chorus of male dancers takes up half the foreground, with a chorus of female dancers on the left. At the center, a guitarist is bent diagonally with his legs doubled up. The orchestra is in the pit in the foreground. *At the Savoy* concentrates on dance couples: one, whose lindy hop is gigantically enlarged, fills the entire top half of the collage. Bearden had truly caught the flavor and tempo of contemporary culture at its coolest in these works. A careful look in stores will show how many book jackets and compact discs are adorned with replicas of Bearden's *Of the Blues* collages.

Finally, the series moves to the music's abstract sounds. *Intermission Still Life,* for example, is a beautiful rendering of clarinets, bass clarinets, and horns at various angles in front of a piece of sheet music on a music stand.

Of the Blues: Second Chorus

The following year, Bearden created a kindred series of mono-prints entitled *Of the Blues: Second Chorus.* Like *Of the Blues,* this new series traced jazz from its folk sources, sacred and secular, to the cities where its major styles evolved (New Orleans, Chicago, New York, Kansas City), then to its performers, and finally to its abstract sounds. Bearden was now exploiting the improvisational possibilities of collage and other media in a way that allowed him to combine a freer, more open approach to his art with his subject—blues improvisation. He began to brush benzine directly onto a plastic plate to "pick out" the color, which he then allowed to splatter and disperse on the paper. The more volatile the mixture of benzine, the more quickly the plate dried.

New Orleans: Storyville/Ragtime Preparations (1975), from *Of the Blues: Second Chorus,* is set in the New Orleans bordello district. There, a latter-day *odalisque,* or concubine, stands in the foreground with her servant primping her. In the background, seen through a doorway, a piano player is absorbed in a ragtime composition. Critics reviewing these monoprints found the synthesis of style and subject (improvisation and jazz) appealing. Said one magazine, "Painterly mist now represents the smoke in the room where the jazzmen play."

The *Jazz* Collages

In spring 1980, Bearden exhibited a series of twenty collages called "Romare Bearden: Jazz." Eighteen of the twenty were executed almost as miniatures—6 by 9 inches (15 by 23 cm) or 9 by 6 inches, like the wonderful *Solo Flight,* a valve trombonist in profile against a hot pink background; or *Storyville,* depicting a bordello piano player, a cigarette dangling from his lips with his hands on the keys and his back to two prostitutes. *Guitar Executive* is another small gem with the clarity and precision of the 1975 *Of the Blues* collages. The two larger works in the *Jazz* series, *Tenor Spot* and *Encore* have the same precision. *Encore,* 18 by 20 inches (46 by 51 cm), shows a jazz singer wearing a colored dress and a white belt, with gardenias on the belt and in her hair, standing full figure next to a curtain with two large white spotlights behind her. It's a stunning piece. In many other *Jazz* series collages, Bearden strove to achieve the free, improvisational effect produced by the oil-on-paper technique he had used in *Of the Blues: Second Chorus.*

In 4/4 Time

Bearden captured this spirit again in his 1981 exhibit *In 4/4 Time*. This series, composed of oils-and-collage on paper, again used the fast-drying method associated with *Of the Blues: Second Chorus*, but added elements of collage. These collaged elements very often consisted of disks, suggesting differently colored spotlights, behind a saxophonist in a work like *Solo Flight*. These tend to create a clearer, more precise line. The pieces that used the fewest collage elements were the most fluid, free, and improvisatory.

In E Sharp, which depicts a bass-fiddle player with his arms wrapped around his bass, his left hand pressing down the string and his right plucking it, is a wonderful example of the work that distinguished this series. The elements of collage are clearly set against the freer, aquamarine background. Bearden has set the browns of the musician's hands and head against the yellow of the front of the bass, the brown of its side, and the blue of his shoulder and sleeve. The strings of the bass are invisible, yet strongly suggested. The F hole of the bass is blue. In theory these colors should not harmonize, yet they harmonize beautifully, making a powerful musical statement.

"Find the Rhythm and Catch It Good"

In the early 1980s, Bearden wrote to a young artist-in-residence who was confused by his latest work. It seemed to violate many of the rules she had been taught about color, harmony, and structure, yet she found it beautiful. How should she proceed? Romare explained that only after a long period of rigorous self-training in the work of Renaissance, Chinese, and African masters was he able to understand that those mysterious elements of structure need only be implied: "How to take the life of the painting and let it, so to speak, breathe. All this, I'm sure, is a matter of being confident that finally everything will turn out all right, because for the most part you struggle along in a deep colorful fog." Bearden advised the artist, "You must become a blues singer—only you sing on the canvas. You *improvise*—you find the rhythm and catch it good, and structure as you go along—then the song is you."

9

North African and Caribbean Light

With the *Odysseus Collages*, exhibited in May 1977, Bearden returned to the Homeric themes of his 1949 watercolors, the *Iliad Variations*, but with an enormous difference in treatment. The *Iliad Variations* had the look of stained glass, their figures were outlined in black ink, almost geometrically, and the handling was cubist. Also, the idea of *Variations* suggested music rather than storytelling. Bearden's twenty *Odysseus Collages* were linked more closely to the narrative line of Homer's *Odyssey* than the 1949 watercolors had been to *The Iliad*. These works had such titles as *The Land of the Lotus Eaters*, *The Cyclops*, *The Sirens' Song*, and *Odysseus and Penelope Reunited*, suggesting the episodes of *The Odyssey*.

However, Romare playfully set forth this epic as if Homer had been a Mediterranean-African bard. The setting was more Moroccan, Algerian, or Tunisian than Greek; all the characters were black; and the light was North Africa's blinding sunlight—

red-hot, sea-blue, and white. Perhaps most of all, the treatment was reminiscent of Henri Matisse's late "cutouts," a dangerous territory for any artist, no matter how original, to explore. Nevertheless, as one critic wrote, Bearden, by the sheer quality of his artistic imagination, had managed to make us see the giants on whose shoulders he stood as partners.

Of the twenty *Odysseus* collages, thirteen are rendered on a large scale and the others on a much smaller scale. Several are among Bearden's best of the decade. *The Sea Nymph*, for instance, is a large work—44 by 32 inches (112 by 81 cm)—with two figures seen as if on land and beneath the sea at the same time. The topmost figure holds on to the white band that unravels from around the nymph as she sinks into the sea. A ship with a single sail on its mast floats on the surface where sea birds fly, while streams of pink, blue, and green surround her.

The Sea God, also 44 by 32 inches (112 by 81 cm), shows a much fiercer being. She is seen in profile, surrounded by fish, wearing an ornate war tunic and holding a spear in one hand and a skull in the other. Her sharp, pointed teeth and large staring eye are most prominent. A white headband holds her tumbling hair in place.

Two of the smaller collages, *Home to Ithaca* and *The Bow of Odysseus,* make powerful statements. The first is a landscape representing Odysseus' ship sailing into harbor. Odysseus stands at the prow surrounded by billowing sails, proudly bearing his shield and spear. *The Bow of Odysseus* is a landscape of suitors about to be slain. *The Return of Odysseus (Homage to Pintoriccio and Benin)* is Bearden's reworking of a much smaller 1969 collage entitled *Homage to Pintoriccio.* It is a forceful, stunning work, showing Odysseus at the right, Penelope at the left, and her loom diagonally in the center. A small bird stands on the rectangular sill of a window that opens on a panorama of mountains and sea.

Romare often spoke about painting as an Odyssean voyage of discovery: "If you're any kind of artist, you make a miraculous journey and you come back and make some statements in shapes and colors of where you were." Bearden had traveled once more, in imagination, and had created a world of heroic myth.

The Obeah's Choice

In 1984, a decade after he had begun to spend half the year on the Caribbean island of St. Martin, Bearden found the heart of its mystery. Perhaps alone among artists, he had been permitted to watch rites of initiation among the Obeah of St. Martin. *Obeah* is defined as a religion, probably of Ashanti (West African) origin, characterized by the use of sorcery and ritual magic. Although Bearden approached rites of magic and sorcery with a healthy skepticism, he also knew that "art goes where energy is," and he had found a great deal of energy in the Caribbean. "It's like a volcano there; there's something underneath that still smolders. People still *believe.* When you stop believing in the gods, they pack their bags and go someplace else!"

Using a volatile mixture of watercolor cut with benzene, which dried on the paper within minutes, Bearden created a striking series of watercolors entitled *Rituals of the Obeah.* Reviewing the series, *New York Times* critic Michael Brenson focused on two key elements of Bearden's work: his handling of the paper and his improvisatory spirit. In various works of the series, Bearden used the silence of the unpainted surface "to light a fire within the paper." The white of the paper in one work was "transformed into dappled rays of sunlight on the clothing and face of a man bewitched." In Brenson's view, "If the Obeah holds such an attraction for Bearden, it is because its mixture of rules, improvisation, trust and sacrifice is characteristic of art-making itself."

Of the eighteen works that comprise the *Rituals of the Obeah* series, *The Obeah's Choice (Le Choix de la Sorcière; Choua Manmbo-A)* is a striking example of this unique mixture. It shows an initiate in the foreground kneeling in profile before an Obeah; the initiate's body is painted solidly in aquamarine, blue, and purple. Just next to the initiate, the form of her body appears in green, and the two figures are joined at the knees. It is as if the Obeah had taken the essence or form of the initiate from her. The Obeah, on the other hand, is depicted almost in geometric outline: her eyes, nose, breasts, and torso are a series of ovals and diagonals spattered with yellow and green. The white of the paper seems to shine through her. Her body has no solidity, which contributes to her mystery, yet the lines defining her are severe. Bearden's explanation of what he had set out to accomplish gives exact definition to the work: "She [the Obeah] has chosen this girl, but she's holding part of her. And this girl can't go away."

Turning to another work, *The Obeah's Dawn*, Bearden remarked on the depth of the myth it drew upon, and the arrogance of the people who believed it. When I asked him what he meant by the word *arrogant*, and if the watercolor depicted a rooster emerging from the Obeah's head and producing the dawn, he responded by asking me how I would feel if I believed that I could make the sun come up. He had ended an article for the *New York Times* with this description of the myth: "An Obeah woman once told me she took the moon before dawn and held it as a locket on her breast and then threw a rooster out in the sky who spun himself in the rising sun." Bearden's concluding line: "*That* is energy."

The Caribbean was another world for Bearden, a new source of energy and a way of getting at another truth. Together with my family, I visited Romare a year later, and saw that world as he led me up the steep stairway of over one hundred stone steps separating his house from his studio high on a hillside in St. Martin. Game cocks strutted outside the glass-enclosed breakfast room of Romare and Nanette's house, their three cats keeping the cocks under careful scrutiny. Halfway up the stone steps, from which lizards darted, I turned around to take in a magnificent world filled with Caribbean light, the bay, islands in the distance, and long-winged birds suspended between sky and sea.

In an article, Bearden describes how, one day, he had watched stonemasons building a wall in St. Martin. Rather than splitting the rocks with powerful swings of their hammers, the workmen tapped at the side of the rocks, and at a certain point, the rocks cracked. When Bearden asked one of the men how this was done, "He explained that by tapping the rock the men were listening for its truth. When they discovered that vein of truth, only a few taps were needed." In much the same way, Bearden had learned to sound the Caribbean for a new vein of truth himself.

10

Celebrating the Victory: The Long Path Home

In 1980, Romare began a series of journeys homeward, both literally and in art. A ten-year retrospective, "Romare Bearden: 1970–1980" opened at The Mint Museum in Bearden's birthplace—Charlotte, North Carolina. Romare traveled home for the opening, telling an interviewer that he had "never really left" Charlotte. Indeed the retrospective's fifty-six collages were a fitting tribute to Bearden's most creative decade, and to the power of his artistic imagination.

Profile/Part II: The Thirties was exhibited a year later, in 1981. This series of collages, with titles and text written in collaboration with Romare's longtime friend Albert Murray, completed the *Portrait of the Artist* begun in 1978 with *Profile/Part I: The Twenties.* Here also, Romare's memories started with Mecklenburg. *Prelude to Farewell,* for instance, was a large 4- by 3-foot (122- by 91-cm) collage showing a young woman at the bath, a grandmother figure in attendance, and a train steaming across the countryside, seen through a window above a coal stove. The narrative read: "She came to the depot in her best dress to see me off. As the train began to move she ran alongside blowing kisses." *The Pepper Jelly Lady* depicts a woman in a courtyard with a rooster facing her. The narrative read: "The trains in the stories she told always ran North." So Romare's early memories were about departure from the people and countryside he loved. As he put it, in order to give life to memory "you have to go back to where you started to gain insights. Things that aren't essential have been stripped away and the meaning of other things has become clear. . . . My great-grandfather's garden, the lady who sold pepper jelly from her basket, and Liza, the little girl I played with, all left a great impression on me."

"The memories are just there; they're just really with me"

In Romare's studio, some years later, I asked him how a series of collages was born in his imagination. "Well," he said, "the memories are just there; they're just really with me. It's strange, the memories are there." Romare kept a small reproduction of Vermeer's famous work, *The Concert,* where he could see it easily. "You see the Vermeer up there on the wall? I'll say, 'Well I saw something like this; this used to be so-and-so.' Because I guess art is made from other art. Yes, I've been in places like this; I've gone in with the same kind of stillness, and the light coming in from this source. Those people [of Vermeer's time] moved on, and the people from Mecklenburg have come in there."

Profile/Part II: The Thirties began with Mecklenburg. Then it skipped over the Pittsburgh years, and continued with the Harlem Bearden remembered from his college years and his

Three Folk Musicians
1967
Collage on canvas board
50 x 60 in.
(127 x 152 cm)

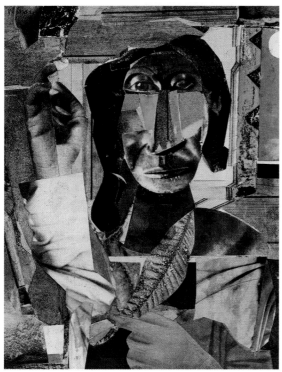

Conjur Woman
1964
Collage of paper and
synthetic polymer paint
9 ¼ x 7 ¼ in.
(23 x 18 cm)

Conjur Woman as an Angel
1969
Mixed media
29 x 23 ½ in.
(74 x 60 cm)

Delilah
(Samson and Delilah)
1974
lithograph
36 x 28 ⅛ in.
(91 x 71 cm)

The Block
1971
Collage of cut paper and
synthetic polymer paint on masonite
6 panels
48 x 216 in.
(122 x 549 cm)

Carolina Shout
1974
Collage with
acrylic and lacquer
37½ x 51 in.
(95 x 130 cm)

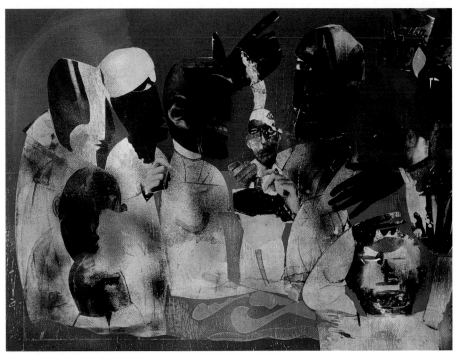

New Orleans Ragging Home
1974
Collage with acrylic and lacquer
36⅛ x 48 in.
(92 x 122 cm)

Wrapping It up at the Lafayette
1974
Collage with acrylic and lacquer
44⅛ x 36 in.
(112 x 91 cm)

One Night Stand
1974
Collage with acrylic and lacquer
44 x 50 in.
(112 x 127 cm)

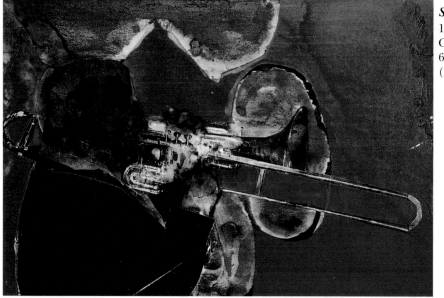

Solo Flight
1979
Collage
6 x 9 in.
(15 x 23 cm)

The Sea Nymph
1977
Collage
44 x 32 in.
(112 x 81 cm)

The Obeah's Choice
(Le Choix de la Sorcière; Choua Manmbo-A)
1984
Watercolor
30 ⅛ x 22 ⅜ in.
(77 x 57 cm)

Artist with Painting and Model
1981
Collage
44 x 56 in.
(112 x 142 cm)

The Piano Lesson
1983
Collage and watercolor
29 x 22 in.
(74 x 56 cm)

Quilting Time
1986
Glass tesserae (mosaic)
113 $\frac{11}{16}$ x 167 $\frac{1}{2}$ in.
(289 x 425 cm)

experiences as a young artist. *Artist with Painting and Model* is a large 44- by 56-inch (112- by 142-cm) collage Bearden created for *The Thirties* series. In it, he remembered how rough it had been for him to get started and how good it felt once he found his true subject matter. In the collage, Bearden the artist stands relaxed, one arm resting on an easel that holds his 1941 gouache on brown paper, *The Visitation.* At the other side of the easel stands a black model, her shapely back to the viewer. On the floor beneath the easel is a preparatory sketch of the same model. In a one-sentence story, on the back of the collage, is Romare's memory: "Every Friday Licia used to come to my studio to model for me upstairs above the Apollo Theater."

Other Harlem scenes like *Uptown Sunday Night Session* and *Slapping Seventh Avenue with the Sole of My Shoe* re-created nightspots and musical duels. *Sitting in at Barron's* carried the narrative: "When you sat down at the keyboard you knew very well you would play only so long as you kept Willie the Lion Smith, J. P. Johnson, Luckey Roberts, and Fats Waller interested in what you were doing." The most striking collage for me was *Uptown Manhattan Skyline: Storm Approaching.* As if Bearden had transposed *Prelude to Farewell* to the north, he depicted a grandmother figure holding an umbrella above a young girl on a Harlem roof, the sky blazing with the light and darkness of the approaching storm.

Bearden continued to work in many different media—collage, watercolor, lithography, silkscreen or serigraph, and mosaic mural. His visual work lent itself to diverse forms of artistic expression—dance, film, book, newspaper, magazine and record illustration. In 1977, for instance, the Alvin Ailey American Dance Theater used Bearden watercolors as maquettes, or source artworks, for the set and costumes of the ballet *Ancestral Voices.* In 1982, the Ailey Theater adapted a Bearden artwork, *The Bridge*, as a scrim or transparent curtain for choreographer Talley Beatty's dance, *The Stack-Up*.

Thirty Bearden watercolors accompanied the opening sequences of the John Cassavetes film *Gloria* (1980). Bearden also designed book covers for Albert Murray's novel *Train Whistle Guitar* (1977), and Dizzy Gillespie's autobiography *To Be or Not to Bop* (1978). In 1983, the Limited Editions Club published Derek Walcott's *Poems of the Caribbean*, accompanied by Bearden watercolors and a Bearden lithograph. Bearden works appear on record albums and compact discs with music by such jazz greats as singer Billie Holiday, alto saxophonist Charlie Parker, percussionist Max Roach, and trumpeter Wynton Marsalis. In 1986, Bearden and alto saxophonist Jackie McLean performed "Sound Collages and Visual Improvisations" at the Wadsworth Atheneum in Connecticut. Bearden painted as McLean played percussion, piano, and sax.

Baltimore Uproar

It had been clear even before the *Projections* series of 1964 that Romare was a master at handling artistic space: the smallest Bearden original could be enlarged many times with no loss of cohesiveness—the sense that all the elements fit together. Bearden's imposing mosaic mural, *Baltimore Uproar*, which showed a singer with a big band roaring behind her, was unveiled in a Baltimore metro station near Billie Holiday's birthplace in 1983. In 1984, *Pittsburgh Recollections*, a ceramic tile mural, was installed in Pittsburgh for the Allegheny County Light Transit Authority. In 1986, *Quilting Time*, a stunningly beautiful mosaic-tile mural, was installed in the permanent collection of the Detroit Institute of Arts in celebration of its 100th anniversary and as part of a major Bearden retrospective of fifty-seven works spanning four decades, from 1945 to 1986.

"Whatever Intelligence You Have Gets Into Your Hand"

Throughout the years, like a man voyaging homeward, Bearden's art was pulling itself with a force almost as strong as gravity toward his childhood memories of Mecklenburg. Perhaps he was now painting what he could not have painted earlier. The greatest of these series was *Mecklenburg Autumn* (1983), twelve oil paintings with collage. It included a suite of four rich autumn landscapes ending with *December: Time of the Marsh Hawk.* With age and experience, Bearden was able to say, "Whatever intelligence you have gets into your hand."

Romare and I began our regular weekly interviews while he was at work on the *Mecklenburg Autumn* series. Although he did not allow observers to see him actually working on a collage, I had the good fortune to see these collages in different stages of composition from week to week. Sometimes, I saw them go from nothing but a ground of colored paper on masonite board to finished collages, and the process was fascinating. In some of these collages, he stripped away more elements than he allowed to remain and painted a great deal of the surface in oil.

Autumn Lamp, showing a country guitarist with a kerosene lamp above him and his guitar at his side, was a struggle for Romare. When I asked him why it had not come easily, as most of his work did, Romare likened the struggle to jazz: "You do something, and then you improvise." The French impressionist Claude Monet once observed that his predecessor, Edouard Manet, always wanted his canvases to appear to have been painted at a single sitting. Often, though, he would scrape down what he had executed during the day, keeping only the lowest layer. Then he would begin improvising. In this sense, Bearden remarked, for Manet, a painting wasn't ever finished.

This was the way Bearden struggled with *Autumn Lamp*. At a certain point in the composing process, he placed a denim shirt and pants (cut from actual pieces of fabric) on the guitarist, "and then I knew when I put these denim sections in, that it had a kind of set to it." But by the time Romare finished *Autumn Lamp*, the only remaining fabric was a small section of the upper part of the guitarist's shirt surrounding his square chin. His guitar is at rest on his thigh; his long hands are at rest one on top of the other; there is a wise smile on his lips and in his eyes. He—like Romare—has played.

When six or seven of the large collages (often 40 by 30 inches [102 by 76 cm]) in the series had been completed, I asked Romare to talk about one I particularly liked, *The Piano Lesson*. He set it right next to us so that we could see it easily as he talked about it. In the collage, a stern teacher stands over her pupil, her finger pointing, while the young pianist performs, her eyes intent on the keyboard.

I asked him how he had started, and he talked about the colors he had painted directly on the acid-free paper covering the masonite board. Comparing his technique to that used by Goya, Manet, and some of the old masters, Romare remarked that they painted on what they called red or brown bolas ground, allowing this ground to play through in their paintings, sometimes using it for the shadows, sometimes almost leaving it. "I've seen some of Goya's paintings where the underneath ground predominated over half the painting, and then he would, say, weave in a certain blue color here and then develop those things that he wanted to be highlighted." Bearden placed himself in the same tradition: "So I let the ground play through. And then what I put on there—the things I lay down—I try to put in proportion to the actual size—in the same ratio."

As for the elements he lay down, Romare made it clear that these included cloth, actual wood, paint, and ornamentation meant to make the atmosphere of a Southern parlor come alive (the metronome, the picture on the wall, the little stained-glass windows, the lamps, the sideboard). Other things, such as a Singer sewing machine and a china lamp, he found in the advertisements of a turn-of-the-century Sears Roebuck catalogue.

Later, Romare diagrammed *The Piano Lesson* for me to show how he had gone about establishing the flatness of the picture plane, a fundamental of cubist composition. Romare's lesson shows just how carefully planned the effortless look of the collage was:

> In the overall format of the painting, the A which you see here, this rectangle, is pretty much in the same ratio as the entire work. Since I depicted a piano that was making a thrust from the left part of the picture, moving on to a kind of perspective toward the right, I had to compensate for that dark area back of that kind of a box rectangle of the piano, to hold it on the flat surface. The rectangle is completely flat, and tips into the box and tends to hold the piano back into the flat picture plane. Now C is a movement in the drapes that moves through the piano onto the teacher's dress. You might say this is all one continuing movement down, from the drapes right on through the teacher—a straight flat movement.
>
> Now at the bottom of the piano, there is a rug. And the rug is set into a rectangular relationship that encloses the teacher and moves across to the young girl. This, I'll call it D, also holds the pic-

ture flat to the picture plane. There is another movement: the end of the back of the chair on which the young girl sits, which again is straight up and moves again to hold the flat picture plane. The drape on the far side, which comes down to the picture, is curvilinear and picks up the curves in the drape to the left of it (I'll put two arrows to show that).

There is a picture, or a mirror, above the piano, and again, it's in the same overall ratio as the entire picture itself. I think these are the main aspects. Coming out of the drape on the right-hand side there is a little cabinet, I'll call that E, that again accentuates the up-and-down movement of the picture. There is a baseboard which is in the same movement directly across this black line; this black movement is in back of the piano, you see, if we trace it across, which again holds to the flatness of the picture.

So I think you'll see without going any further what I'm talking about, trying to get volume through the contrasting movements of planes while still trying to hold the flatness of the picture plane.

Mecklenburg: Morning and Evening

In 1985, the demands on Bearden's energy and creativity were intense. Preparations for a major retrospective at the Detroit Museum of Arts were nearly simultaneous with the creation of fourteen collages for an exhibit entitled "Mecklenburg: Morning and Evening."

Jefferson Cooley's Evening Guitar is a powerful collage from the *Morning and Evening* series. It is a portrait in reds, yellows, deep

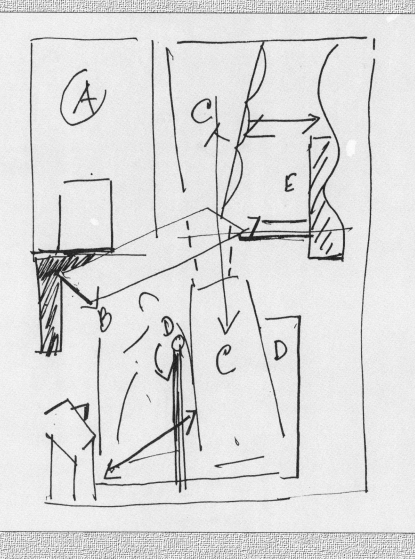

In this diagram of The Piano Lesson, *Bearden shows the relationships of objects in the collage to each other and to the flatness of the picture plane— all crucial elements of cubist composition.*

blues, and whites of a country guitarist in profile. His face, however, is an African mask. *Wednesday Evening* is another work in which the outsize, masklike face of the subject takes up fully a third of the picture's surface.

Quilting Time

One day in 1985 at Romare's Long Island City studio, he showed me a lovely work he called *Quilting Time*. A collage of paper on board roughly 20 by 32 inches (51 by 81 cm), it would be installed in the permanent collection at the Detroit Institute of Arts, not far from the huge mosaic-glass mural 113 $^{11}/_{16}$ by 167 $^{1}/_{2}$ inches (289 by 425 cm) for which it served as the maquette or model. The mural would be unveiled at the opening of the Bearden retrospective "Origins and Progressions" in September 1986.

Quilting Time contains eight figures. A group of five figures on the left is focused on the brightly colored quilts covering the laps of two seated women, one of whom looks directly toward a guitar player. The group surrounding the guitar player is completed with a woman holding a baby. Altogether, the figures form an arc, with the sun's disk (also an arc) just left of center. Off to the right, above a gray fence, a white songbird is set off by tropical foliage. "I've concocted a nice quilt," Romare said. "Everything else is gray. . . . And the little white bird picks up the white needed at that spot. Then you've got the man's sleeve; the girl in the middle with her white, and then the white of the dress of the big lady on the right, with the white curtain. The white is carrying right across."

Romare then made a line drawing to illustrate this movement and hand-wrote a commentary next to it: "In a work of a long format, such as *Quilting Time*—the "whites" or very light accents, moving across the picture plane can (1) give an expansion to the work—as the eyes of the onlooker move from one light area to the next—(2) aid in uniting all the elements in the painting."

In a second line drawing, Romare identified the linear rhythms moving throughout the work: "These are the principal lines of force again attempting to unify the painting. The movements go in and out of the garmented figures—so everything in the painting—figures, foliage and objects [is] conceived as a continuum."

Romare then made a third and final line drawing that focused on the three figures surrounding the quilt. It demonstrates the integration of several figures in a single unified design. He wrote this commentary: "The two ladies working on the quilts are so conceived in the work, that if the quilts were not there, the quilts, so to speak, could be the dresses of both women. The lady I marked A has a quilt that touches the young girl in gray, and I made a dark blue area in her dress carrying through the rhythm of the quilt and in addition giving body and credence to the woman quilting." As if to sum up this integration, Romare said, "Everything is part of something else." It reminded me of the quote from William Wordsworth that Romare kept on the wall of his studio. It read, "All things are one and related."

Like so much of the work Romare created, *Quilting Time* was a combination of Mecklenburg memories and quilting bees he had seen as a child there. "It may have come to me in selecting a quilting bee as my subject," Bearden stated, "that the technique had something to do with my own use of the medium of collage. After all, working in collage was precisely what the ladies were doing."

Romare felt too exhausted to make the trip to Detroit for the opening of the retrospective. But in January and February 1987, Romare, Nanette, and their three cats were able to travel to warm, sunny St. Martin, where Romare wrote his dealer and old

These line drawings based on Bearden's collage and mosaic-glass mural Quilting Time *illustrate the movements, rhythms, and integration of figures into a unified design.*

friend Arne Ekstrom, "I'm happy to report that I'm making good progress. In fact, I'm able to negotiate the 109 steps leading up to my studio—with a little help from a cane. . . . And I feel very well." In fact, days after returning to New York in early March, Bearden summoned André Teabo/Thibault to Canal Street to discuss a new series of big collages on the theme of jazz. Thibault had been Bearden's informal student for some years, and the student was about to become the master's assistant.

Bringing It All Back Home

By middle March, with André Thibault preparing the collage boards and the paper backings, Romare began work at the studio. Throughout April and May, they worked steadily and intensely on large collages, bursting with color. *All the Things You Are* is a saxophone player seen in profile, and rendered in bright, sunny yellow and orange watercolor with collage elements interlaced with the watercolors so tightly they can hardly be seen.

By late May 1987, I accompanied Albert Murray to the studio, where he helped Bearden title the works and organize them in a series, as he'd done so often in the past. The first collage he saw depicted a pianist in profile at an upright piano, his large left hand with a wristwatch displayed prominently, a derby cocked down over his head, a cigar in his mouth, a bow tie, and an ornamented vest. His face was a mask, and his entire bearing suggested that when he sat down at the piano, he meant business. He reminded Albert Murray of the master composer and performer Duke Ellington and the emphasis he placed on a unique, sonorous opening chord. Bearden liked that, so Murray suggested the title *Opening Statement* and went on to name the others, placing them in groups moving from jazz soloists to duos, quartets, quintets, and big bands for the show, which was scheduled to open at a Boston gallery in late fall.

Work continued until mid-June. The following week, the Beardens traveled to Washington, D.C., where Romare was awarded the National Medal of Arts by President Ronald Reagan. On the evening before the White House ceremony, there was a down-home touch to the outdoor dinner as Romare stole away with fellow recipient Ella Fitzgerald for some *real* food—Southern fried chicken.

By early July, Bearden wrapped up work for the moment and prepared to journey with Nanette to St. Martin. When they returned to New York in September, the work for the Boston show was nearly complete. Then, on a day in which he was in great pain and the work had been slow and difficult, Bearden told Thibault how gravely ill he was. Against all odds, Bearden and his assistant persevered, producing work that was quite beautiful and new. Perhaps this last great burst of creative energy came from Bearden's knowledge that he was fighting the clock.

In early November, work resumed on the striking *Moonlite Prelude,* in which a locomotive steams across a long, high trestle, its engine's light piercing the night sky. In the foreground, a guitar player, cigarette in his mouth, plays the blues beside a nude lying on a blanket, her back to the viewer.

In mid-December, work began on the first of two complementary collages with watercolor. *Eden Noon* (first dubbed "the hundred-animal piece") shows a nude bathing in a pond surrounded by a playful fantasy landscape composed of egrets, a blue dove, a gigantic bullfrog, and various fish. *Eden Midnight* shows a nude, now bathing in a stream alongside a waterfall, a twinkling star in the night sky, and a landscape filled with mythological, perhaps prehistoric creatures, a gigantic butterfly, an alligator, and a dinosaur. Taken together, the two *Eden* collages are extraordinary works of art. Their subject matter combines elements Bearden had used throughout his career (the nude bathing, the stream, the waterfall) with a mythological, fantastic element that had never before appeared in his work. Bearden continued to surprise: it was as if he were trying to outpaint death. And he kept on painting until four days before entering the hospital for the last time.

Romare Bearden died of cancer at the age of seventy-six on March 12, 1988. As the poet Chateaubriand wrote, "Every man carries within him a world composed of all that he has seen and loved, and it is to this world that he returns incessantly." In his art, with its great themes of black life, ritual and ceremony, Caribbean sea and sky, jazz players and blues singers on his canvases, Romare Bearden gave his special world to all of us.

Chronology

1911	*September 2.* Romare Howard Bearden born in Charlotte, North Carolina, to Richard Howard and Bessye Johnson Bearden.
1914–15	Beardens relocate to New York City.
1917	Bearden enrolls at P.S. 5, New York, New York; later transfers to P.S. 139.
1919–20	Bearden family spends year in Moose Jaw, Saskatchewan, Canada.
1920–21	Bearden spends year in Pittsburgh, Pennsylvania.
1925	Graduates from P.S. 139.
1925–27	Attends De Witt Clinton High School, New York, New York.
1929	Graduates from Peabody High School, Pittsburgh, Pennsylvania.
1935	Receives B.S. degree in mathematics from New York University; works as a cartoonist.
1936–37	Studies life-drawing and painting with George Grosz at the Art Students League, New York; joins "306," an informal association of black artists living in Harlem, most of whom were also members of the Harlem Artists Guild.
1938	Enters New York City Welfare Department as caseworker.
1940	Begins painting in tempera on brown paper, primarily Southern scenes; takes a studio on 125th Street.
1942	*April.* Enlists in the U.S. Army, 372nd Infantry Division.

1944	*February 13–March 3.* Solo exhibition, "Ten Hierographic Paintings by Sgt. Romare Bearden," at G Place Gallery, Washington, D.C.
1945	*May.* Discharged from Army as sergeant.
	June. Solo exhibition, "The Passion of Christ," at G Place Gallery, Washington, D.C.
	October 8–27. Twenty-four works from "The Passion of Christ" shown at Samuel M. Kootz Gallery (first one-artist exhibition in New York gallery).
	December 17. *He Is Arisen* (1945) acquired by the Museum of Modern Art, New York (first work to be purchased by a museum).
1946	Resumes duties as caseworker for New York City Welfare Department, continuing to serve intermittently until 1949.
1947	*February 24–March 15.* Solo exhibition, "New Paintings by Romare Bearden," at Samuel M. Kootz Gallery, New York; eighteen paintings inspired by Rabelais's *Gargantua and Pantagruel* shown.
1948	*November 9–25.* Solo exhibition, "The Iliad Variations," at Niveau Gallery, New York (sixteen works shown).

1950	Goes to Paris on the GI Bill to study philosophy at the Sorbonne; later travels to Nice, Florence, Rome, and Venice.
1951	Returns to New York; paints intermittently but concentrates on songwriting; has many songs published.
1952	Resumes work for New York City Welfare Department; continues this work until 1966–67.
1954	Collapses on street; hospitalized for a month, having suffered a nervous breakdown.
	September 4. Marries Nanette Rohan; returns to painting, working in an increasingly abstract style.
1956	Moves into studio/living space on Canal Street, New York.
1958	Paintings now almost exclusively nonfigurative.
1960	*January 20–February 19.* Solo exhibition at Michel Warren Gallery, New York (nonfigurative paintings shown).
1961	Begins to reintroduce figurative elements in paintings. *April 6–25.* Solo exhibition, "Bearden," at Cordier-Warren Gallery, New York; continues to show nonfigurative paintings. *May–June.* Travels in Europe with Nanette, visiting Paris, Florence, Venice, Genoa, and parts of Switzerland.

October 27–January 7, 1962.
Works included in "The 1961 Pittsburgh International Exhibition of Contemporary Paintings and Sculpture" at the Carnegie Institute, Pittsburgh, Pennsylvania.

1963   *July.*
Spiral group formed, meeting initially in Bearden's studio; group later opens a gallery; friend Reginald Gammon suggests photographing collages and enlarging them.

1964   *June.*
Collages seen by Arne Ekstrom, who encourages Bearden to make a series for fall exhibition.

October 6–24.
Solo exhibition, "Romare Bearden Projections," at Cordier & Ekstrom, Inc., New York, includes collages from the Projections and their photo-enlargements (twenty works shown).

1965   *October 1–31.*
Solo exhibition, "Projections," at Corcoran Gallery, Washington, D.C.

March 4–27.
Four collages entitled *Panel on Southern Theme* included in an exhibition at the National Institute of Arts and Letters.

May 25.
Receives grant from the National Institute of Arts and Letters; ten collages shown in "Exhibition of Work by Newly Elected Members and Recipients of Honors and Awards."

Official retirement from New York City Welfare Department. Bearden continues to do some work into 1967.

1967   *October 16–November 5.*
Codirects with Carroll Greene, Jr., "The Evolution of Afro-American Artists: 1800–1950," sponsored by the City University of New York, the Harlem Cultural Council, and the New York Urban League, in the Great Hall of City College, New York.

1968   *November 25–February 9, 1969.*
Solo exhibition, "Romare Bearden: Paintings and Projections," at the Art Gallery, State University of New York at Albany.

1969   *June.*
Coauthors *The Painter's Mind* with Carl Holty.

December.
First exhibition at Cinque Gallery in Joseph Papp's New York Public Theater at 425 Lafayette Street, New York.

1970   *June.*
Receives grant from Guggenheim Foundation to write a book on the history of Afro-American art; it is completed by his coauthor, Harry Henderson, as *A History of African American Artists from 1792 to the Present* in 1993, five years after Bearden's death.

December 3–January 30, 1971.
Patchwork Quilt (1970) included in exhibition "She" at Cordier & Ekstrom, Inc., New York; collage acquired by the Museum of Modern Art.

1971   *March 23–June 9.*
Major solo retrospective exhibition, "Romare Bearden: The Prevalence of Ritual," organized by the Museum of Modern Art, New York.

1972	Coauthors *Six Black Masters of American Art* with Harry Henderson; elected to the National Institute of Arts and Letters.
1973	Begins summering on the island of St. Martin in the Caribbean.
1974	*March 28–April 28.* Solo exhibition, "Romare Bearden: The Prevalence of Ritual, Martinique and Rain Forest," at Cordier & Ekstrom, Inc., New York (twenty-four works shown). Portfolio of five silkscreens, *The Prevalence of Ritual.*
1975	*January 20–May 6.* Three works included in exhibition, "The Barnett-Aden Collection," Anacostia Neighborhood Museum, Washington, D.C. *February 14–March 15.* Solo exhibition, "Romare Bearden: Of the Blues," at Cordier & Ekstrom, Inc., New York. *September 5–October 26.* Solo exhibition, "Mysteries: Women in the Art of Romare Bearden," at the Everson Museum of Art of Syracuse and Onondaga County, Syracuse, New York.
1976	*February 11–March 14.* Solo exhibition, "Of the Blues: Second Chorus," at Cordier & Ekstrom, Inc., New York.
1977	*April 27–May 28.* Solo exhibition, "Romare Bearden: Odysseus Collages," at Cordier & Ekstrom, Inc., New York.

1978   Receives the Frederick Douglass Award at the thirteenth annual awards celebration.

November 10–December 16.
Solo exhibition, "Romare Bearden Profile/Part I: The Twenties," Cordier & Ekstrom, Inc., New York.

1980   Executes thirty watercolors for opening sequences in *Gloria,* a Columbia Pictures film; *Bearden Plays Bearden,* a film presentation of the Institute of New Cinema Artists, is produced by Third World Cinema.

March 29–April 19.
Solo exhibition, "Romare Bearden: Jazz Collages," at the Sheldon Ross Gallery, Birmingham, Michigan.

October 12–January 4, 1981.
"Romare Bearden: 1970–1980," a ten-year retrospective organized by the Mint Museum in Bearden's hometown of Charlotte, North Carolina (fifty-six collages shown).

1981   *May 6–June 6.*
Solo exhibition, "Romare Bearden Profile/Part II: The Thirties," Cordier & Ekstrom, Inc., New York.

October 1–November 7.
Solo exhibition "In 4/4 Time: Oil and Collage on Paper," Cordier & Ekstrom, Inc., New York.

1983   Illustrates *Poems of the Caribbean* in collaboration with Derek Walcott; designs Baltimore Metro Line Mural, Baltimore, Maryland.

November 12–December 17.
Solo exhibition "Mecklenburg Autumn: Oil

Paintings with Collage," Cordier & Ekstrom, Inc., New York.

1984   Designs Pittsburgh Transit System mural, Pittsburgh, Pennsylvania.

August 30–September 22.
Solo exhibition "Watercolors from St. Martin," Sheldon Ross Gallery, Birmingham, Michigan.

November 14–December 15.
Solo exhibition "Rituals of the Obeah," Cordier & Ekstrom, Inc., New York (eighteen watercolors shown).

1986   *September 16–November 16.*
Solo exhibition "Romare Bearden: Origins and Progressions," the Detroit Institute of Arts, Detroit, Michigan—major retrospective including fifty-seven works in various media, including the mosaic mural *Quilting Time*.

September 23–November 1.
Solo exhibition "Mecklenburg: Morning and Evening," Cordier & Ekstrom, Inc., New York (eighteen watercolors with collage shown).

1988   *January 23–April 3.*
Solo exhibition "Riffs and Takes: Music in the Art of Romare Bearden," North Carolina Museum of Art, Raleigh, North Carolina.

March 12.
Bearden dies, following several months' illness with bone cancer.

1989   *May 11–June 10.*
"Romare Bearden: A Memorial Exhibition" held at ACA Galleries, New York—exhibition includes fifty-five works in various media executed between 1941 and 1988.

For Further Reading

Bearden, Romare. "Rectangular Structure in My Montage Paintings." *Leonardo 2*, (1969): 11–19.

Bearden, Romare, and Carl Holty. *The Painter's Mind: A Study of the Relations of Structure and Space in Painting.* New York: Crown, 1969.

———, and Harry Henderson. *A History of African-American Artists: From 1792 to the Present.* New York: Pantheon Books, 1993.

———. *Six Black Masters of American Art.* Garden City:Doubleday, 1972.

Berman, Avis. "Romare Bearden: 'I Paint out of the Tradition of the Blues.'" *Art News.* December 1980.

Brown, Kevin. *Romare Bearden.* New York: Chelsea House, 1995.

Campbell, Mary Schmidt. "History and the Art of Romare Bearden." *In Memory and Metaphor: The Art of Romare Bearden 1940–1987.* Exhibition Catalog, The Studio Museum in Harlem. New York: Oxford, 1991.

———. "Romare Bearden: A Creative Mythology." Ph.D. Dissertation. New York: Syracuse University, 1982.

Driskell, David C. *Two Centuries of Black American Art.* New York: Knopf, 1976.

Ellison, Ralph. "Romare Bearden: Paintings and Projections." *The Crisis 77* (March 1970): 80–86.

Gelburd, Gail, and Thelma Golden. *Romare Bearden in Black and White: Photomontage Projections*, 1964. Exhibition Catalog. Whitney Museum of American Art. New York: Harry N. Abrams, 1997.

Murray, Albert. "The Visual Equivalent of the Blues." *In Romare Bearden: 1970–80.* Exhibition Catalog. Charlotte, NC: Mint Museum, 1980. See also Dore Ashton, "Romare Bearden" and *Listing of Works* 1970–1980, compiled by Jane McKinnon in this catalog.

Schwartzman, Myron. "Of Mecklenburg, Memory, and the Blues: Romare Bearden's Collaboration with Albert Murray." *Bulletin of Research in the Humanities* (Summer 1983): 140–61.

———. *Romare Bearden: His Life and Art.* New York: Harry N. Abrams, 1990.

Sims, Lowery S. "The Unknown Romare Bearden." Art News (October 1986): 116–20.

Tomkins, Calvin. "Putting Something Over Something Else." *The New Yorker* (November 8, 1977): 53–58.

Washington, Bunch M. *The Art of Romare Bearden: The Prevalence of Ritual.* New York: Harry N. Abrams, 1973.

Index

Page numbers in italics indicate illustrations

About the Author

Myron Schwartzman is Professor of English at Bernard M. Baruch College of the City of New York. He met Romare Bearden in 1978, when Bearden's "Profile/Part I: The Twenties" was exhibited at the Cordier & Ekstrom Gallery in New York, and then spent much of the next ten years meeting with Bearden each week at his Canal Street and Long Island City studios. During a memorable week in 1985, the interviews continued at Bearden's hillside studio in St. Martin. Schwartzman published the definitive authorized biography of Bearden, *Romare Bearden: His Life and Art* (Harry N. Abrams), in 1990.

Schwartzman, a jazz pianist by avocation, shared a love of jazz and literature with Bearden, who taught Schwartzman how to see his art with a fresh eye. Schwartzman has written widely about Bearden and James Joyce in *ArtForum, The Bulletin of Research in the Humanities, Callaloo, James Joyce Quarterly,* and *Modern Fiction Studies.* He played piano with painter Larry Rivers's East 13th Street Band from 1978–86, touring in the United States and the Dominican Republic.

A sketch by Romare Bearden of the author photographing the artist's work